Russian Colonialism 101

ISBN 978-617-7948-49-9

For years, Ukrainian journalist Maksym Eristavi has been mainstreaming the global awareness about the legacy of Russian colonialism. A few days before Russia launched a full-scale invasion of Ukraine, he started a Twitter thread listing all Russian colonial invasions over the last century and highlighting one specific pattern that they all went by. The post has gone viral and is now dubbed the "mother of all Russian colonialism tweets". Together with a group of Ukrainian artists, Eristavi transformed it into an illustrated pocket guide to the 48 most recent invasions of Russian colonialism — to bring everyone's attention to a pattern of serial behavior by the largest colonial empire.

The first publication is prepared with the support of the MOCA NGO and the Ukrainian Emergency Art Fund in collaboration with the Sigrid Rausing Trust. Some illustrations created during the illustrative workshop for the book "Russian Colonialism" have been donated to the Ukrainian Museum of Contemporary Art (UMCA).

© ist publishing, 2024
© Maksym Eristavi, 2022
© Sergiy Maidukov, Alisa Gots, Nikita Kravtsov, Nataliia Kozeko, Danyl Shtangeev, Natasha Steshenko, Ave Libertatemaveamor, illustrations, 2023

All rights reserved.

publishing

Russian Colonialism 101

How to Occupy a Neighbor and Get Away with It:
An Illustrated Guide
Edited by Maksym Eristavi

The empire will fall,

*You can find a list of sources used, as well as a QR code with all Internet links, at the end of the book.

I lost my sleep two days before the genocide of my people began.

For the Ukrainian in me, it was my generational genocide trauma that kicked in, putting me on instant alert. This was not the first time my people had faced an impending mass murder.

For the journalist in me, I just had to deal with my anxieties the best way I knew how — by telling a story and providing context to the catastrophe that was about to happen. I've been trying to mainstream global awareness about Russian colonialism for almost a decade, and I couldn't believe that the impending full-scale invasion of Ukraine was perceived abroad as something unprecedented and new. So, during those sleepless nights, I started a Twitter thread mapping every instance of Russian colonial invasions in the last 111 years. I wanted to illustrate, simply and powerfully, that Russia's upcoming assault on Ukraine is a centuries-long, copy-paste colonial job. Throughout different regimes using various ideological labels, Moscow uses the same pretext and strategy to enforce its colonial domination in the Russian neighborhood: gaslight, invade, exterminate [1, 2]*. It has deployed various combinations of it for centuries, but the Kremlin perfected the final formula at the beginning of the 20th century. Russia hasn't changed the strategy since then.

I started the thread with a picture of the devastated city of Grozny in Chechnya (or Nóxçiyn Respublik Içkeri) that was razed to the ground by Russia in the 2000s as revenge for an attempt by the indigenous nation to leave the empire. It was a kind of visual provocation to encourage everyone to imagine what could happen to Ukraine if the world did not react and stand up to Russian colonialism. I finished the thread days after February 24th, 2022, realizing, with utter horror, that Ukrainian cities from Mariupol, Kyiv, and Kharkiv to Chernihiv, Sievierodonetsk, and Bakhmut, were starting to look exactly the same as the 2000s graveyard of Grozny.

Since then, the thread, dubbed "The Mother of All Russian Colonialism Threads" [3], became viral and grew into a storytelling hub.

Now, together with a group of wartime Ukrainian artists and illustrators led by Sergiy Maidukov, we turn "The Mother of All Russian Colonialism Threads" into a piece of defiant art and storytelling. We are not attempting to serve you with acade-mic work, historical analysis that untangles nuanced and messy events, or a piece of investigative journalism. It is not an exhaustive list of all war and mass murder atrocities Russian colonialism and imperialism resulted in during this period, either. This book is a conversation starter that I hope will serve as an eye-opener for some of you. It is based on publicly-available information anyone can access — despite Russia spending enormous amounts of resources to rewrite, hide, and erase memory about its colonial crimes [4]. Moreover, you don't need to know much about the topic in advance to find this guide useful and illuminating.

Our mission is to connect the dots between various atrocities committed in the name of Russian imperial supremacy and bring everyone's attention to a pattern of serial colonial behavior by Moscow [5]. Our hope is to enlighten more people around the world about generations of freedom fighters, the believers in democracy and justice who resisted and pushed back against Russian invasions over and over. There was not a single land that welcomed Russian colonial boots. Millions of indigenous voices were silenced trying to speak out about crimes of Russian colonialism committed against them: their stories and their names matter.

Ukrainians are not the only people who have suffered continuously from unprovoked Russian aggression and land stealing. But we believe that the cycle of unpunished Russian imperialism and colonialism has to stop with us.

Tannu-Tuva
1911–1944

- Gaslight: stoking division
- Invade: to protect / to civilize
- Exterminate: cultural erasure / settler colonialism

The indigenous Siberian nation of Tyvan leaves the Chinese colonial empire and declares independence in 1911. In the name of the safety of ethnic Russians, Russia invades the Uryankhay Republic and absorbs it in 1914 using Russian-sponsored petitions signed by local nobility as a formal excuse [1]. The occupation collapses amid the 1917 revolutions, and in 1921, the Tyvan nation declares independence once again. Russian colonialism, now with the communism label, limits Tannu-Tuva's sovereignty: defense and foreign policy decisions are transferred to Moscow, while the swarm of Russian diplomats and advisors increasingly influence local politics [2]. They empower local pro-Russian paramilitary forces and assist them with a coup d'etat in 1929 to install a puppet regime. Mass murder of political and religious elites follows, as well as cultural erasure and destruction of the traditional livestock economy. Moscow fuels Russian settler colonialism: Tyvans go from making up 80% of the population in 1918 to 57% in 1959 [3]. After discovering rich mineral deposits, Russia illegally annexes Tannu-Tuva in 1944, using a formal request by its own puppet regime [4, 5].

Exhibit 1

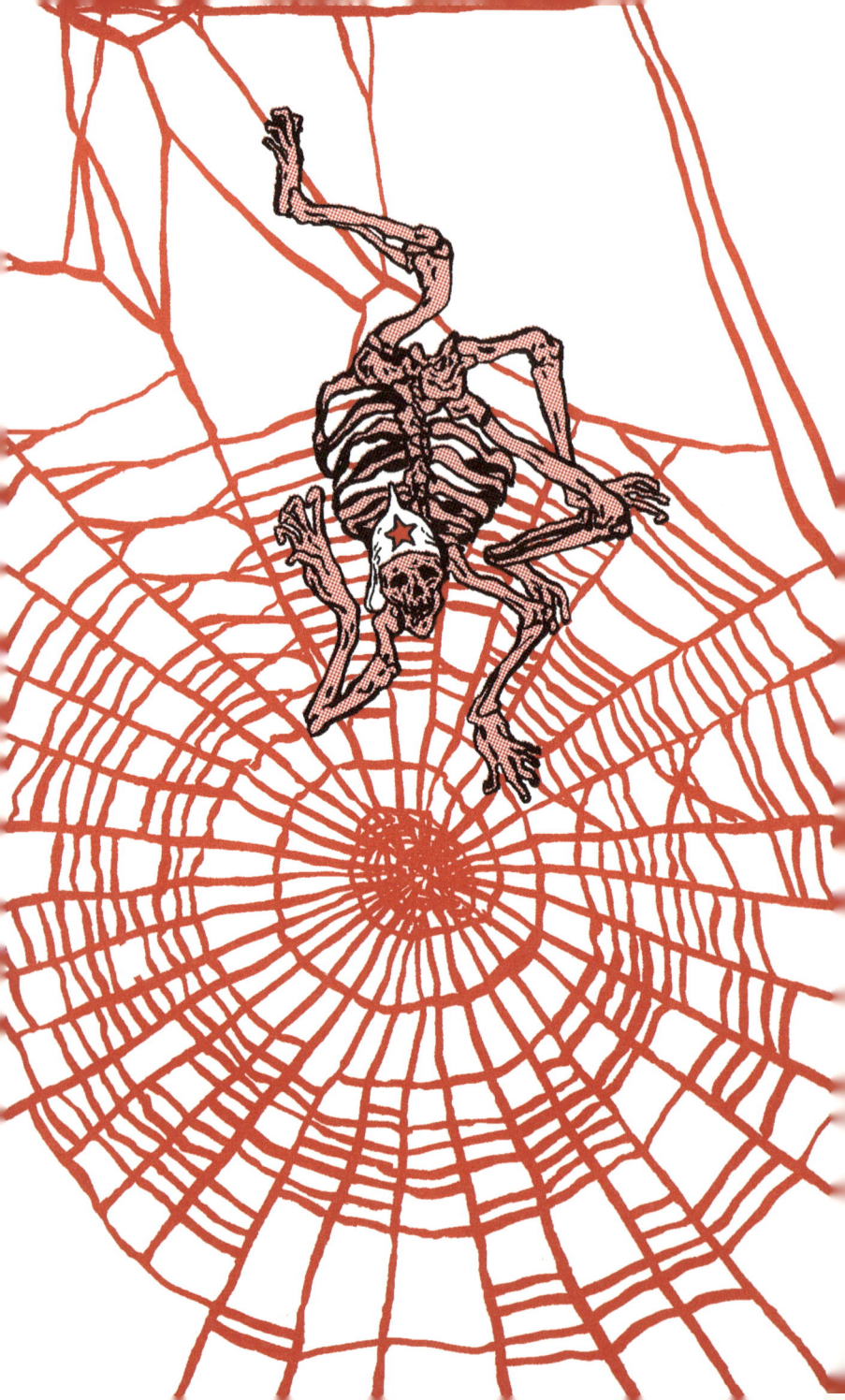

Iran
1911–1946

- Gaslight: stoking division
- Invade: to protect
- Exterminate: mass terror

After facing centuries of meddling by Western and Russian colonialism, Iran is trying to reassert independence. Russians conspire with the British to invade the country to "protect it from violence". Russia shells ancient cities to the ground, rapes, loots, and mass murders to crush Iranian democratic and anti-colonial uprising [1]. It sponsors settler colonialism, too [2]. In 1917, the regime in Russia changes, but Russian colonialism doesn't. Now with the communism label, Moscow sets up a puppet state in northern Iran to justify expanding occupation [3]. Iranians push the Russians out in 1921 but are forced to sign a peace deal that includes a clause allowing Russia to invade once again if it believes foreign troops using the country as a staging area for an invasion of the Soviet Union. Moscow uses the planted loophole to invade the country in 1941 "to protect itself from an invasion". During the occupation, the Kremlin fuels the internal divide, loots local resources, sets up puppet "people's republics" in the name of Azerbaijani and Kurdish minorities, and starts stealing Iranian oil. However, Russian troops return home under concerted international pressure in 1946 [4, 5, 6].

Exhibit 2

Central Asia 1916–1934

- 🚩 Gaslight: identity erasure / stoking ethnic division
- 🔴 Invade: to protect / civilize
- 🔻 Exterminate: genocide / cultural erasure / settler colonialism

Indigenous people of Central Asia try to leave Russian colonialism [1, 2] after two hundred years of colonial rule that involved violent military conquest, the corruption of local institutions, and the expropriation of the best lands for Russian settlers [3]. Central Asian nations revolt against serving in the Russian imperial army during WWI and Russian settler colonialism. They demand sovereignty and envision democracies rooted in education, Islam, and equality. Qazaqs declare a secular Alash republic. The secular and multinational democracy of Turkestan unites Uzbeks, Kyrgyz, Tajiks, Qazaqs, and other nationalities. Khiva and Bukhara monarchies also join the anti-colonial pushback. Russia sets up puppet states and sends troops to "protect them from ethnic violence" and to "civilize them out of feudalism" [4]. Bukhara, one of the oldest cities in the world, is ruthlessly bombed. Millions get slaughtered across the region in pogroms and ethnic cleansing [5], as well as in the controlled famine that follows, known as the Asharshylyk genocide [6]. Moscow battles the anti-colonial Basmachi uprising in Central Asia [7, 8, 9] for almost two decades but eventually crushes it by 1934 [10, 11, 12].

Exhibit 3

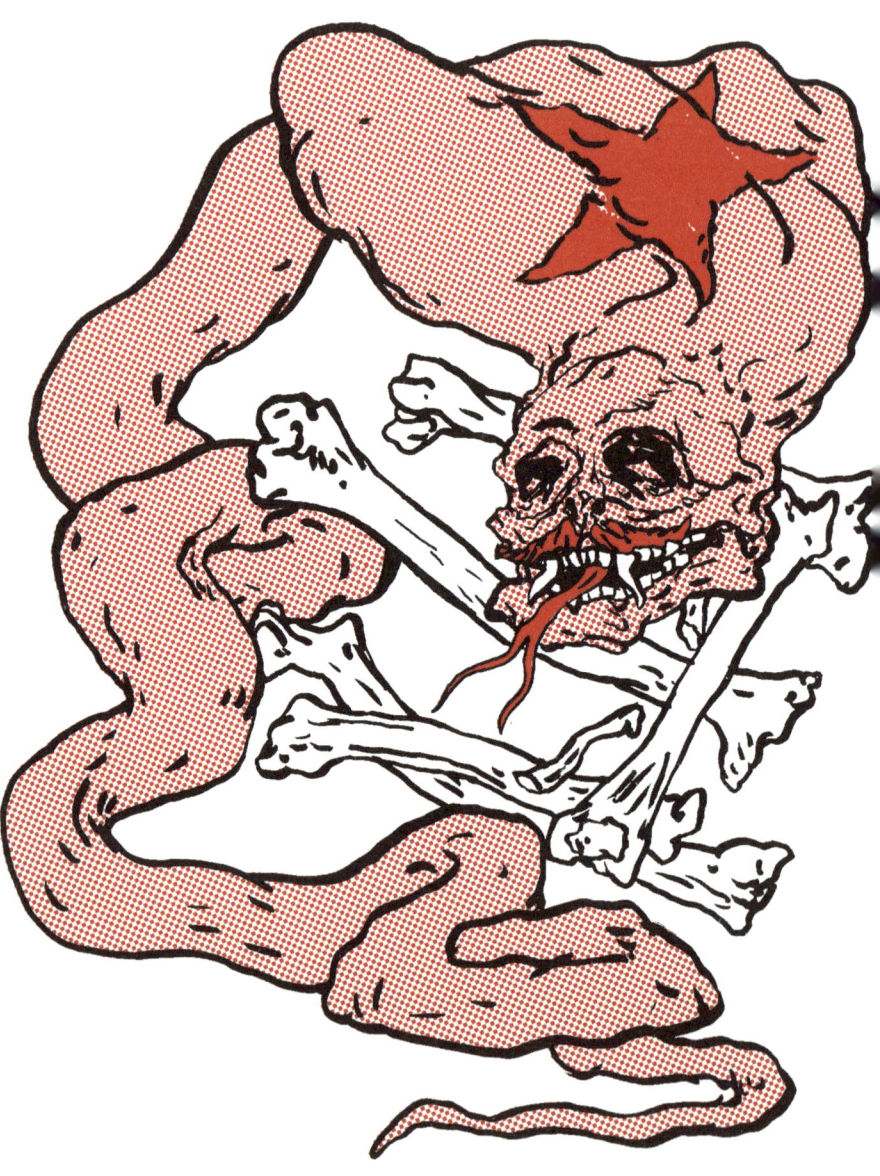

Ukraine
1917–1953

- Gaslight: stoking division / disinformation
- Invade: to protect itself
- Exterminate: genocide / Russification / settler colonialism

Amid the 1917 revolutions in Russia, Ukrainians leave the Russian colonial empire and proclaim an independent state [1]. The Russian empire regroups, now with the communism label, and launches a wave of terrorist attacks over the years, stoking internal political division, and eventually re-occupies Ukraine by 1921 [2]. The rest of Europe lets Russia have it. The Kremlin targets Ukrainian farmers, the country's largest class and the base of intensifying anti-colonial sentiment, with mass asset seizures, terror [3], and deportations [4]: over 500,000 fall victim to the terror during 1930–1932, with more than 200,000 [5] joining them when Russia expands colonial control over Western Ukraine in 1944–1953. During 1932–1933, a man-made famine known as the Holodomor genocide [6] kills between five and seven million — every fifth Ukrainian. The entire generation of the Ukrainian intellectual elite, known as the Executed Renaissance [7, 8, 9], is wiped out in the late 1930s. During World War II, Russia uses Ukrainians as cannon fodder in the war with Nazi Germany: Ukraine loses approximately ten million people, the deadliest price paid for the war amongst all Allied countries [10].

Exhibit 4

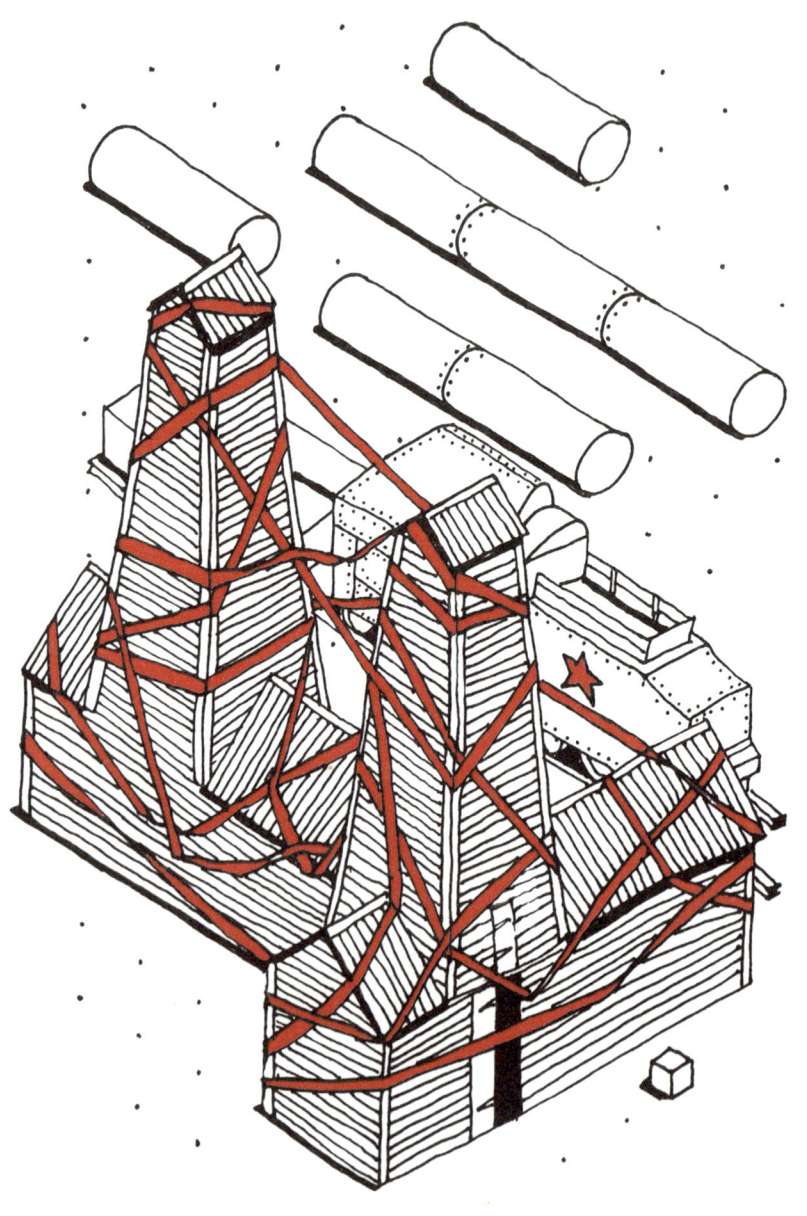

Azerbaijan
1917–1920

🚩 Gaslight: stoking division / disinformation
🚩 Invade: to protect / stop violence
🚩 Exterminate: mass terror

      Following the 1917 revolutions in Russia, Azerbaijanis leave the Russian colonial empire. In 1918, they found the third Muslim democratic republic in history. Azerbaijan also elects a parliament in free elections based on universal suffrage that includes women, making it one of the first countries in the world and the very first majority-Muslim nation to do so. The Russian Empire regroups, now with the communism label, and starts eyeing the rich oil fields of Azerbaijan to fund the recolonization of the lands it lost after recent revolutions. The Kremlin manufactures disinformation campaigns about mass murders and ethnic pogroms in Azerbaijan and invades "to protect and stop the violence". Tens of thousands are slaughtered in the following terror [1], and Azerbaijan remains occupied [2] for the next 70 years [3].

Exhibit 5

Armenia
1917–1920

🔴 Invade: to protect

Following the 1917 revolutions in Russia, Armenians leave the Russian colonial empire. The nation is devastated by the Türkiye-conducted genocide and several wars with neighbors. Nevertheless, Armenians declare a democratic republic [1]. The country grants full voting rights to women — one of the first in the world to do so. Armenians also elect several female parliament members, setting a precedent ahead of most European countries. By late 1920, a young democracy is sandwiched between two creeping invasions from Türkiye and Russia. Moscow stokes a divide within the country, instigates a failed coup, and in late 1920 the Russian army invades the country "to protect and liberate it". In practice, it means dissolving the republic and the Russian occupation of Armenia [2].

Exhibit 6

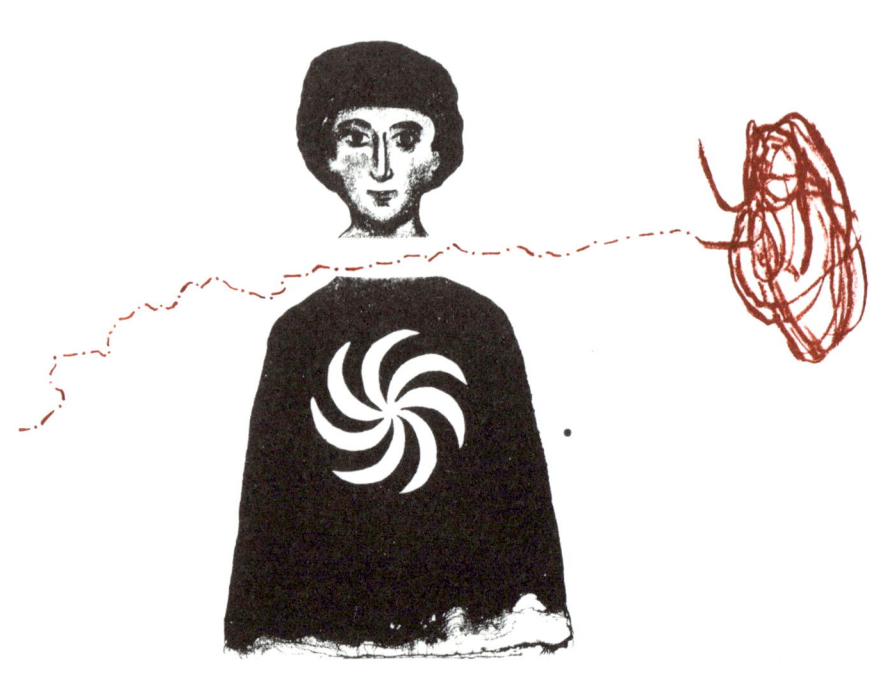

Sakartvelo (Georgia) 1917–1924

- Gaslight: disinformation / stoking ethnic division
- Invade: to protect / stop violence
- Exterminate: ethnic cleansing

One of the oldest nations in Europe, Sakartvelo, has been under Russian occupation since the 19th century. Following the 1917 revolutions in Russia, Georgians (or self-called Kartvelians) leave the Russian colonial empire and declare independence. They form one of the first liberal and plural democracies in Europe with equal human and political rights [1]. That includes women who co-write the Georgian Constitution and are elected as parliament members [2]. The Russian empire regroups, now with the communism label, and a young Georgian democracy ends up encircled by Russian-occupied lands. The West supports Sakartvelo in words but refuses to send arms. Foreign embassies flee. Moscow stages ethnic violence and invades to "protect itself" [3]. The empire executes thousands of Kartvelians [4] and deport approximately 20,000 more in the ethnic cleansing that follows [5, 6, 7].

North Caucasus 1917–1945

- Gaslight: disinformation / stoking ethnic division
- Invade: to protect / stop violence
- Exterminate: genocide

Following the 1917 revolutions in Russia, several indigenous nations in the northern Caucasus leave the Russian colonial empire. The peoples of Dagestan, Chechnya (Noxçiyçö), Ingushetia (Ghalghajče), Ossetia (Iryston), Karachays (Qaraçaylıla), Balkars (Malqarlıla), Circassians (Adıgəxər), and Abkhaz (Apsny) are among the oldest nations in the world and have been under Russian colonial oppression for centuries. Nevertheless, the region remains one of the strongholds of the fiercest resistance to Russian colonialism. The nations form a confederation of The Mountainous Republic of the Northern Caucasus [1], uniting almost twelve million people. Some European nations recognize the state, but most refuse in the face of reemerging Russian colonialism — now with the communism label. Moscow stokes ethnic divisions, invades the republic, and re-occupies it. The Kremlin deploys a series of genocides [2] in the following decades to pacify the colonized region [3]. The deportation of entire nations of Chechens [4] and Ingush to Central Asia in 1944 kills between 200,000 and 400,000 alone: around every third of each population [5].

Exhibit 8

Bashqortostan 1917–1921

- Gaslight: stoking division
- Invade: to protect
- Exterminate: mass terror

Following the 1917 revolutions in Russia, the Bashqort (Başqorttar), an indigenous Muslim nation of Ural, decides to leave the Russian colonial empire. They form a democratic government — one of the first in the Muslim world, an army and a provisional parliament [1]. The Russian empire regroups, now with the communism label, and starts stoking internal divisions, terrorizes, mass murders, and kidnaps members of the Bashqort parliament [2]. In the Baymak massacre of early 1918, The Russians slaughter several Bashqort MPs and some of the nation's army command [3], inspiring more anti-colonial guerrilla movements in the region [4]. However, Bashqortostan ends up sandwiched by the Russian civil war. Soviet Moscow lures the Bashqort into a military union with fake promises of preserving their democracy, then absorbs the republic by early 1919 [5] and pillages it for rich natural resources in the decades that follow.

Exhibit 9

Estonia
1917–1920

- Gaslight: stoking division
- Invade: to protect
- Exterminate: failed, Russia is kicked out

After 200 years of Russian colonial rule, which included multiple ethnic cleansing campaigns, Russification, and outright slavery, Estonia leaves the Russian colonial empire amid revolutions in Russia and founds a democratic republic in 1918 [1]. Moscow gets its colonial grip back, now with the communism label, assembles pro-Russian Estonian paramilitary forces, a puppet Estonian leadership, and invades to "protect Estonian opposition" [2]. The Russians quickly occupy more than half of the country. Despite facing a far superior army in terms of manpower, the Estonian resistance grows fiercer. British and Finnish help arrives at a crucial moment [3]. Despite the ongoing Russian invasion, the country manages to have its first-ever democratic election, form a government [4], launch progressive reforms, and build up an effective, modern army. Estonian soldiers not only push Russians out of Estonian borders but also chase them deep into Russian territory, helping to liberate parts of neighboring Latvia from the invaders too. Moscow agrees to a peace deal with Estonia in 1920 [5].

Exhibit 10

Qırım-Crimea
1917–1944

- Gaslight: stoking division
- Invade: to protect
- Exterminate: genocide / settler colonialism

The indigenous nation of Crimean Tatars (Qırımlı) [1], has been under Russian colonial rule since the 18th century and suffered from ethnic cleansing and settler colonialism [2]. Amid the 1917 revolutions in Russia, Qırım leaves the Russian colonial empire and forms the first democratic Muslim state with equal suffrage for everyone. A gene- ration of young and progressive Qırımlı leads the anti-colonial revival. 32-year-old lawyer and writer Noman Çelebicihan is elected as the first president of the Crimean People's Republic. He dreams of a country where ethnic, linguistic, and political diversity is guaranteed. The Russian empire regroups, now with the communism label, and invades Qırım to "protect the opposition". Local Qırımlı, Ukrainian, and ethnic Russian communities mobilize in United Crimean Headquarters to defend themselves from the Kremlin invasion, but they are outnumbered. Mass terror, looting, and ethnic pogroms follow. Russians lure recently resigned President Çelebicihan for peace talks and murder him, dumping his body into the Black Sea [3]. Moscow sets up a puppet Crimean state [4]. Survived Qırımlı leadership petitions for military help from newly-independent Ukraine. Kyiv pushes Moscow out of Qırım at first, but Russians re-invade it after re-colonizing Ukraine in 1921 [5]. They retaliate with mass stealing of Crimean foods, which results in the starvation of approximately a third of Crimean Tatars (76,000) [6]. Moscow also punishes anti-colonial uprisings in the following years by deporting [7] the entire nation [8] to Central Asia in 1944 [9] — every second Qırımlı dies in this genocide [10]. This decreases their share of the Qırım population from 88% in 1795 to 25% in 1926 and just 0.7% in 1979 [11, 12].

Don and Kuban' 1917–1920

- Gaslight: stoking division
- Invade: to protect
- Exterminate: genocide

Ukrainian Cossacks were self-ruled anti-colonial rebels and the founding people of the first Ukrainian democracy [1, 2]. After a catastrophic peace deal with Russia in the 17th century, some are forced to resettle in the Kuban region. Amid the 1917 revolutions in Russia, the Ukrainians of Kuban and Don leave the Russian colonial empire, forming the Kuban People's Republic and the Don Republic, uniting several million people [3, 4]. Both democracies claim convoluted and overlapping authority in an ethnically diverse region of the North Caucasus and Eastern Ukraine [5]. The first Kuban government has three indigenous ministers out of ten. Many deputies in the Kuban parliament are also non-Ukrainians [6]. The Russian empire regroups, now with the communism label, and claims that the Cossack states are a foreign conspiracy on Russian land, that the Kuban and Don Ukrainians are actually Russians, and invades both republics. Cossacks push the invasion back and appeal before the Paris Peace Conference for recognition [7] but get rejected as inconvenient voices "provoking Russia". Then the Russians, both communists and monarchists, fuel disinformation to wedge a chasm between Don and Kuban Ukrainians and Kyiv. They follow up with Mass terror, killing Ukrainian political and intellectual leadership or forcing it into exile. Mykola Ryabovil, a 33-year-old Kuban People's Republic's parliament speaker, is assassinated by Russians hours after publicly vowing to form a wide anti-colonial military union in the region. In the decades that follow, Kuban Ukrainians suffer from aggressive Russification, and the Holodomor genocide kills up to 80% of some of their communities [8]. Moscow also exterminates approximately 70% — or 700,000 — Don Cossack people [9].

Exhibit 12

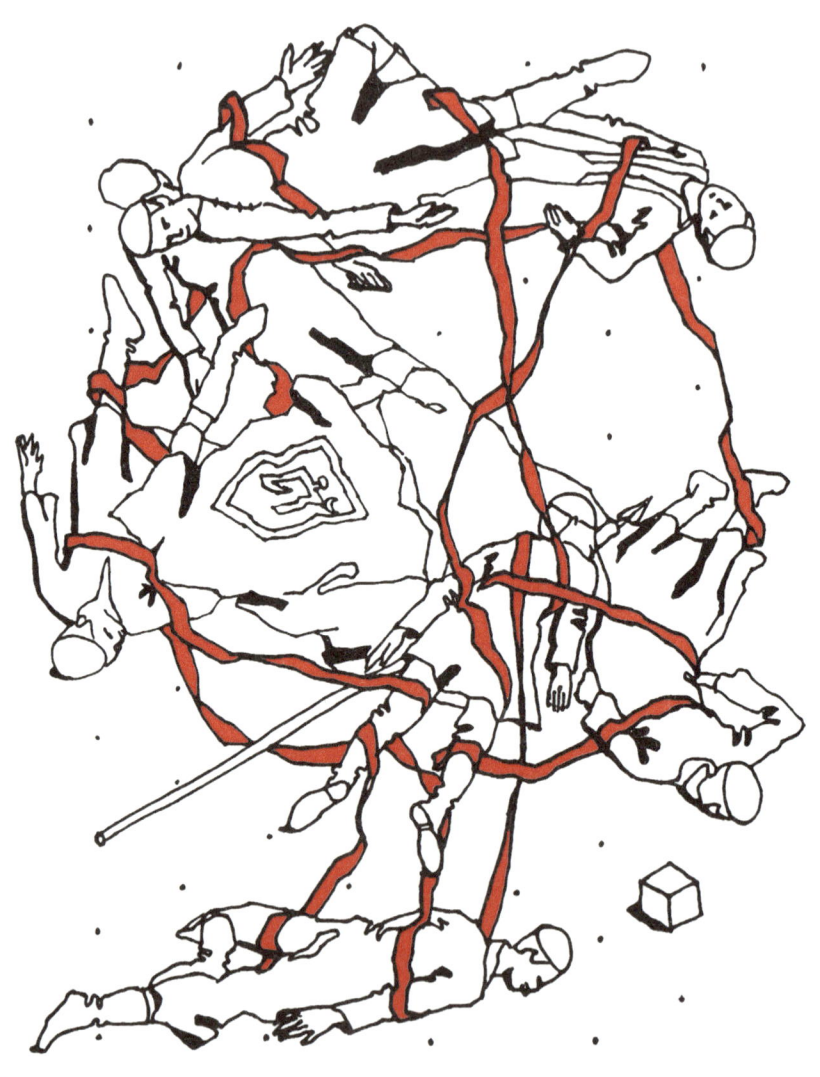

Idel Ural
1917–1918

- Gaslight: stoking division
- Invade: to protect
- Exterminate: ethnic cleansing

The indigenous Muslim and Turk nations of Ural have been under Russian colonial rule for centuries. Amid the 1917 revolutions in Russia, they leave the Russian colonial empire to set up a democratic parlia- ment [1] and a government tasked to form a federation [2] of seven indigenous nations (Tatar, Bashqort, Chuvash, Mari, Erźat, Mokšet, and Udmurtjos), uniting seven million people. The Idel Ural (Idel-Ural ölkäse) [3] founders have a progressive and trailblazing vision of a Muslim political nation bound by democracy and equal rights. The Russian empire regroups, now with the communism label, and assures the Idel Ural leaders that Russia is not an enemy — especially since a proto-federa- tion commands a massive army of 60,000 soldiers [4]. Then, the Kremlin launches propa- ganda and disinformation campaigns, stoking political and ethnic divides. Right before Idel Ural is ready to proclaim independence in early 1918, Russians declare a competing puppet state within the same borders and start kidnapping members of the state-forming assembly and military leadership of Idel Ural. The indigenous state still proclaims inde- pendence on March 1st, 1918 but collapses in several weeks amid Russian terror and occupation [5]. In the following years, Russian colonialism starves almost a third of the local population to death [6].

Exhibit 13

Belarus
1917–1921

- Gaslight: stoking division
- Invade: to protect
- Exterminate: ethnic cleansing

Since the Russian occupation in the 19th century, Belarus has suffered Russification and the ban of the Belarusian language [1] and culture [2]. Amid the 1917 revolutions in Russia, Belarusians leave the Russian colonial empire and declare independence in March 1918 [3, 4]. Russians and Germans, who are at war, want to turn Belarus into a buffer zone instead. At first, the Germans invade. Despite this, Belarus forms a government and an army [5]. Neighboring newly independent Ukraine, which also fights for its survival, becomes a key ally of the Belarusian Demo- cratic Republic, sending food to the country to keep Belarusians from starving [6, 7, 8]. Estonia, Finland, and Lithuania also recognize Belarus, but the rest of the West refuses — independent Belarusians are too inconvenient and "provoke Russia" [9]. The Russian empire regroups, now with the communism label, and, when the German occupation collapses, creates a puppet Belarusian government and invades Belarus to "liberate" it. In the final battle for Belarusian independence, a small Belarusian army resists an enormous Kremlin onslaught for over a month on a heroic suicide mission, known as the Slutsk Uprising [10]. The resistance collapses on the last day of 1920. Over the next three decades, the Kremlin will deploy a combination of mass terror, controlled starvation, and using Belarusians as cannon fodder in World War II to wipe out four million — one third — of the Belarusian population [11] and hijack their national identity [12].

Moldova
1917–1953

- Gaslight: stoking division
- Invade: to liberate
- Exterminate: ethnic cleansing

Moldova has been colonized by Russia since the mid-19th century and went through aggressive Russification [1]. Amid the 1917 revolutions in Russia, the Moldovans leave the Russian colonial empire and declare independence. A young democracy struggles to establish full order, sandwiched by Ukrainian liberation wars and Russia's creeping occupation of southern Ukraine. Chișinău requests military protection from neighboring Romania, which becomes a polarizing public issue [2]. The Russian empire regroups, now with the communism label, fuels the political and ethnic divide, finances pro-Russian paramilitary forces, and invades Moldova to "liberate it". The Romanians push the Russians back but also take control over the young republic through formal "unification" [3]. The Kremlin persists in creating a compe- ting puppet state on the Moldovan border, which doesn't even have a Moldovan-majority population and keeps instigating uprisings inside Moldova [4]. As part of a colonial pact with Nazi Germany, Russia reoccupies Moldova in 1940. Overall, during this period, tens of thousands of Moldovans fell victim to mass murders, deportations, and controlled famine by Russian colonialism [5, 6]. Colonial policies also meddled with Moldovan identity and rooted ethnic and territorial divides that haunt the country to this day.

Exhibit 15

The Kalmyks-Xal'mgud 1917–1943

- Gaslight: stoking division
- Invade: to liberate
- Exterminate: genocide / settler colonization

The indigenous Kalmyk-Xal'mgud people are the only Buddhist-majority nation of Europe. Since the late 18th century, they have been colonized by the Russians. Amid the 1917 revolutions in Russia, the Xal'mgud decide to leave the Russian colonial empire. They form a temporary military government headed by 30-year-old Danzan Tundutov and join an anti-colonial coalition of Ukrainian Cossack and Northern Caucasian newly independent states. Moscow gets its colonial act together, now with the communism label. It assembles terrorist squads of local convicts, extremists, and Russian deserters to take over the Kalmyk capital, Astrakhan. After days of street warfare, they drive the government out. In mid-1918, and with Ukrainian help, Tundutov liberates the capital, but then in 1919, Russians re-occupy it [1]. Moscow punishes the Xal'mgud people with two controlled famines in 1922 and 1933, killing every third in the nation [2, 3]. Kalmyks keep revolting, and Moscow goes for a "final solution" and deports [4] the entire nation in 24 hours to North Asia. Every fifth, or over 16,000, die [5]. The empire dissolves the Xal'mgud region, replace all local toponyms with Russian and repopulate with settler-colonists. Around 350,000 Kalmyks lived on their own lands in the early 18th century. By 1959, only 100,000 remained. When Moscow allowed Xal'mgud to return from the deportation [6], they made up just 35% of the population of their own region [7].

Exhibit 16

Buryad Mongolia 1917–1937

- Gaslight: stoking division
- Invade: to liberate / to civilize
- Exterminate: ethnic cleansing

The indigenous Siberian nation of Buryats-Buryaad has been colonized by the Russians since the 17th century [1]. Amid the 1917 revolutions in Russia, it leaves the Russian colonial empire and proclaims the State of Buryad-Mongolia [2, 3]. The nation forms a provisional government [4] but gets sandwiched by the civil war between Russian communists and monarchists. A new state has to share overlapping authority over the same territory with a military regime of Russian settler-colonists. The latter infiltrate the Buryad-Mongolia government, stoke political and ethnic divide, and disband it by absorbing it into a Russian-controlled regime in 1921. The Communist invasion fully takes over the Buryad territories by 1923 to "civilize it out of feudalism". Mass terror, destruction of the traditional livestock economy, Russification and cultural erasure follow. Moscow crushes any following attempts at local anti-colonial rebellions. Tens of thousands [5] are slaughtered or become refugees by 1937 [6].

Latvia
1918–1920

- Gaslight: stoking division
- Invade: to protect
- Exterminate: failed, Russia is kicked out

After decades of anti-colonial awakening [1], Latvia leaves the empire amid the 1917 revolutions in Russia [2]. Moscow regroups, now with the communism label, finances marginal pro-Russian political and paramilitary forces, and invades to "protect Latvian opposition" [3]. Russia creates a competing puppet Latvian government and manufactures a "civil war" narrative to legitimize the invasion. Mass murder and starvation follow on the occupied lands. Russians steal and ship away most of the Latvian industrial infrastructure. At one point, the Latvian government is forced to govern from a ship in the sea for almost two months [4]. The West doesn't want to upset Russia or empower Germany, which also eyes Latvia, and therefore is hesitant to help. Latvians recruit Poles, Estonians, and Brits and kick the Russians out in 1920 [5]. But Latvia is denied international recognition until it signs a humiliating peace agreement with Russia [6]. This contributes to the eventual collapse of democracy and makes the country easy prey for the Soviet-Nazi colonial pact of 1939 [7].

Exhibit 18

Lithuania 1918–1920

- Gaslight: stoking division
- Invade: to protect
- Exterminate: failed, Russia is kicked out

A nation with one of the oldest statehood histories in Europe, Lithuania has spent over a century under Russian colonial rule [1] that included ethnic cleansing [2] and the ban of the Lithuanian language [3]. In 1918, Lithuanians leave the Russian colonial empire and re-establish independence as a democratic republic. The empire regroups, now with the communism label, finances unpopular pro-Russian political forces, assembles a puppet Lithuanian government, and invades to "protect it". The Russians capture the capital Vilnius and occupy around 20% of the country's territory, terrorizing, looting, and blackmailing locals into paying hefty war taxes. With the help of German volunteers, nationwide mobilization, and rapid military reforms, Lithuanians break the invasion's momentum. Overwhelmed by the resistance and a parallel pushback in the invasion of Poland, Russia asks for a peace treaty in July 1920 [4]. It recognizes Lithuania's independence in exchange for granting Soviet forces unrestricted movement during the war against Poland. Just two days after signing the deal, Russians violate it by occupying the Lithuanian capital. The Kremlin plans a coup to overthrow the Lithuanian government and recolonize the republic [5]. But heavy losses in Polish, Latvian and Estonian invasions force Russians to leave Lithuania [6].

Exhibit 19

Karelia-Karjala 1918–1922

- Gaslight: stoking division
- Invade: to liberate
- Exterminate: ethnic cleansing

After Finland leaves the Russian colonial empire in 1917, the neighboring indigenous nation of Karelians (Karjalaižet) gets inspired to do the same — it has been occupied by Russia since the 18th century [1]. Karjala declares independence and forms a temporary government of the Republic of Uhtua (or East Karelia) in June 1918. Many Finnish volunteers cross the border and join the anti-colonial uprising in solidarity, but Finland keeps a distance at first. The Russian empire regroups, now with the communism label, and falsely paints the resistance as a foreign incursion. Moscow invades in May 1920 and drives the Karelian government into exile. The country's resistance army, called Forest Guerrillas [2], keeps fighting for freedom for almost two more years and secures some military backing from Finland [3]. But they are outnumbered by Russian invasion troops, which crush them by February 1922. Tens of thousands of Karelians become refugees and flee to Finland. Karelian indigenous culture suffers from erasure [4] and Russification [5, 6]. Moscow turns the region into a massive concentration camp for political prisoners from all over the empire [7] and inflicts irreversible environmental ruin.

Exhibit 20

The Tungus Republic 1918–1924

- Gaslight: identity erasure
- Invade: to protect / to civilize
- Exterminate: ethnic cleansing

The indigenous Ewenki people are one of the most ancient Northern Asian nations and have been colonized by Russia since the 18th century. They have suffered from exploitation, identity erasure, and aggressive Russification. The communist phase of Russian colonialism brings a new wave of terrorism: a ban on centuries-old traditions, razing to the ground, peaceful settlements and taxing every aspect of indigenous livelihoods to "civilize them out of feudalism". In May 1924, the Ewenki nation rebels, drives the empire out, and proclaims independence. The provisional government appeals to the League of Nations for assistance and solidarity, but there is none. At first, the Kremlin calls the anti-colonial uprising "a bunch of thugs" but then changes the tactic and lures the Tungus Republic into surrendering with fake promises of autonomy [1]. In the years that follow, Moscow mass murders the people behind the Republic and Ewenki national awakening [2], continues identity erasure [3], pillages natural resources, and inflicts irreversible environmental ruin.

Exhibit 21

Sakha
1918–1927

- Gaslight: stoking division
- Invade: to liberate / to civilize
- Exterminate: mass murder / settler colonization

A land with abundant natural resources, Sakha, has been colonized by Russia since the 17th century [1]. Amid revolutions in the metropole, the nation of Sakha leaves the Russian colonial empire in 1918 and declares independence [2]. It gets sandwiched by the civil war between Russian communists and monarchists. Both fuel the internal divide in Sakha and repeatedly invade it. In 1922, Moscow creates a competing puppet Yakut Autonomous Soviet Socialist Republic to claim legitimacy over Sakha lands, but locals keep resisting [3]. In 1927, the Russian empire, now with the communism label, prevails [4]. Mass murders and persecution of Sakha elites follow. The Kremlin erases indigenous spiritual traditions and destroys the traditional economy, which puts locals in economic dependence on the metropole, leaving thousands to die from famine [5]. Moscow also turns the region into a massive prison camp, with 105 gulag camps covering one-third of Sakha's land [6]. The empire builds an extractive economy through settler colonialism: the indigenous population goes from the 90% majority in 1917 to 33% minority in 1989 [7].

Mongolia
1918–1941

- Gaslight: stoking division
- Invade: to protect / to liberate / to civilize
- Exterminate: mass murder

Mongolia is trying to break free of Chinese colonialism [1] and asks for international help. Russian monarchists and communists use the opportunity to hijack and insert themselves into domestic infighting and invade the country in the early 1920s. Russian monarchists do it under the pretense of "defending Mongolia from the Chinese", while Moscow communists aim to "liberate" Mongolia from "feudalism" Russian colonialism, now with the communism label, uses secret diplomacy with China [2] and a wide network of Russian "advisors" infiltrating the Mongolian government [3] to bring the country into full colonial subjugation. Moscow starts handpicking Mongolian leadership, arresting and executing those they don't like, as happened to two Mongolian prime ministers in 1937 and 1941. To solidify Russian colonial hegemony over the country's natural resources, politics, and culture [4], the Kremlin gives the Mongolian leadership explicit instructions for a purge [5] of all potential regime critics. The resulting terror killed around 4–5% of the Mongolian population, or 22,000–30,000 people [6].

Exhibit 23

The Khanty
1931–1933

- Gaslight: identity erasure
- Invade: to protect / to civilize
- Exterminate: mass murder

The indigenous nation of Khanty in Northern Asia has been resisting colonization by Russia for centuries. Aggressive economic exploitation and cultural erasure accelerate during Russian colonialism with the communism label. Throughout the 1920s, Moscow forces the Khanty to abandon the forest lifestyle and move to government-managed settlements. The Kremlin locks the nation into economic dependency to "civilize" it. Authorities kidnap indigenous children en masse and subject them to violent identity erasure. This is coupled with the mass murder of community and spiritual leaders. The nation rebels in the Kazym anti-colonial uprising and demands cultural, self-governing, and economic autonomy. Instead, the Kremlin drowns it in blood, decimating local indigenous villages with aircraft artillery and machine guns [1, 2, 3, 4, 5].

Exhibit 24

The Dolgans
1932

- Gaslight: identity erasure
- Invade: to protect / to civilize
- Exterminate: mass murder / settler colonialism

The indigenous nation of the Dolgans (Dulğan) in in Northern Asia has been colonized by Russia for centuries. Economic exploitation and cultural erasure accelerate during Russian colonialism with the communism label. Throughout the 1920s, Moscow is excessively taxing every aspect of indigenous livelihoods, taking away reindeer herds that have sacral value for a Dolgan, and terrorizing the community to "civilize it". The nation rebels in an anti-colonial uprising in 1932, but Moscow dismisses the resistance as "bandits". The Dolgans recognize the Kremlin's authority but demand autonomy. The resistance's leadership appeal to the League of Nations for solidarity, but one of the rebel leaders, Roman Barkhatov, is assassinated by Russians while attempting to deliver the telegram. Moscow lures the Dolgans into a ceasefire with fake promises but later murders uprising leaders and anyone resisting colonial policies [1]. Local reindeer herding is almost eradicated. Together with expanding settler colonialism and invasive industrialization [2], it brings economic, environmental, and cultural ruin to the Dolgan communities [3].

Exhibit 25

The Nenets
1934–1943

- Gaslight: identity erasure
- Invade: to protect / to civilize
- Exterminate: mass murder / settler colonialism

The indigenous Arctic nation of Nenets (Nenəj Nenəče) has resisted colonization by Russia for centuries. Economic exploitation and cultural erasure accelerate during Russian colonialism with the communism label. Throughout the early 1930s, Moscow targets the Nenets through the seizure of reindeer herds and land, murder of spiritual and community leaders, and mass kidnapping of indigenous children to boarding schools where they are subjected to violent identity erasure. Later, the Kremlin starts enlisting indigenous men in the army and uses them as cannon fodder in World War II. The nation rebels in the anti-colonial Mandalada uprising. The Nenets demand autonomy the end of settler colonialism, and put a stop to economic exploitation. Moscow deploys troops and machine guns against the Nenets, who fight back with vintage rifles or, as in the case of Nenets women, with axes. The surviving resistance is arrested, and many are tortured to death, like the uprising's leader Sergei Noho [1, 2].

Exhibit 26

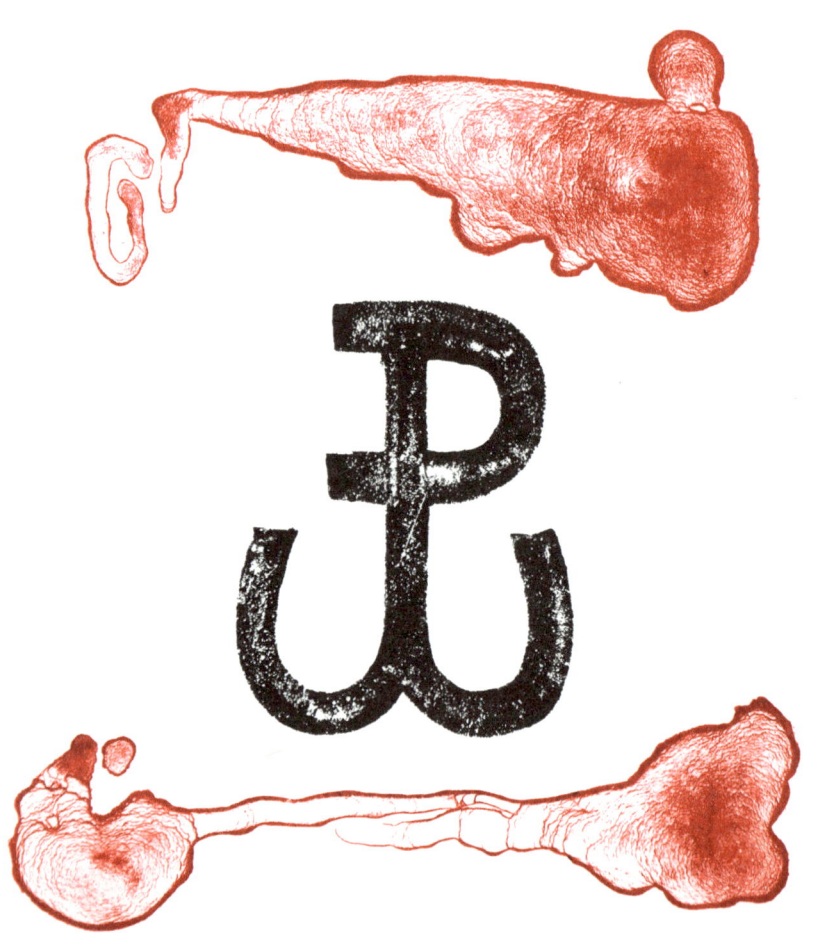

Poland
1937–1947

- Gaslight: stoking division / disinformation
- Invade: to protect
- Exterminate: genocide

Russian attempts to colonize Poland have been on and off for centuries. Planning another one, the Russian empire, now with the communism label, starts with the ethnic cleansing of the Polish population in newly-colonized Belarus and Ukraine. In 1937, Moscow manufactures disinformation about Poles being foreign spies and launches a genocide, slaughtering over 111,000 of them — every fifth Pole living under Russian rule — with the excuse of "protecting" Russia [1, 2, 3, 4]. In 1939, as a facade for a secret colonial deal to divide Europe with Nazi Germany, Moscow claims the protection of ethnic minorities in Poland, invades it, and partitions it up together with Berlin [5]. In the following World War II years, Russian imperial troops kill approximately 150,000 [6], deport over 320,000 [7], and rape up to 100,000 [8] Polish citizens [9]. The Kremlin installs a Soviet satellite regime in Poland by 1945. Tens of thousands of Poles resist Russian occupation in the anti-colonial Wolność i Niezawisłość ("Freedom and Sovereignty") guerillla movement between 1944 and 1953, but most are killed or deported [10, 11]. Russia oversees the falsification of the 1946 referendum [12] and the 1947 parliamentary election to solidify the power of the satellite regime [13]. The international community consents [14].

Finland
1939–1940

- Gaslight: disinformation / accusing of fascism
- Invade: to protect
- Exterminate: failed, Russia is kicked out

The Russian empire, now under the communism label, schemes to recolonize Finland as part of a secret colonial deal with Nazi Germany. In 1939, Moscow creates a puppet statelet — the Finnish Democratic Republic on the Finnish border — and manufactures anti-Finnish disinformation, vows to protect it against the "fascist military clique in Helsinki", and uses it as a front to invade Finland [1, 2, 3]. Russian imperial troops expect an easy victory within several days because the Finnish army is several times smaller and has almost no modern weaponry [4]. However, the plan backfires as the Finnish society mobilizes the largest resistance pushback in the country's history. Finns use smart, non-conventional warfare to break the Russian invasion's momentum [5]. Amid a catastrophic and embarrassing loss of almost 400,000 Russian imperial soldiers and the growing exhaustion of the Finnish resistance, both sides sign a peace treaty that allows Russia to walk away with 10% of the Finnish territory. Finns defend their democracy, but approximately 26,000 are killed by the empire, and 450,000 lose their homes [6, 7].

Exhibit 28

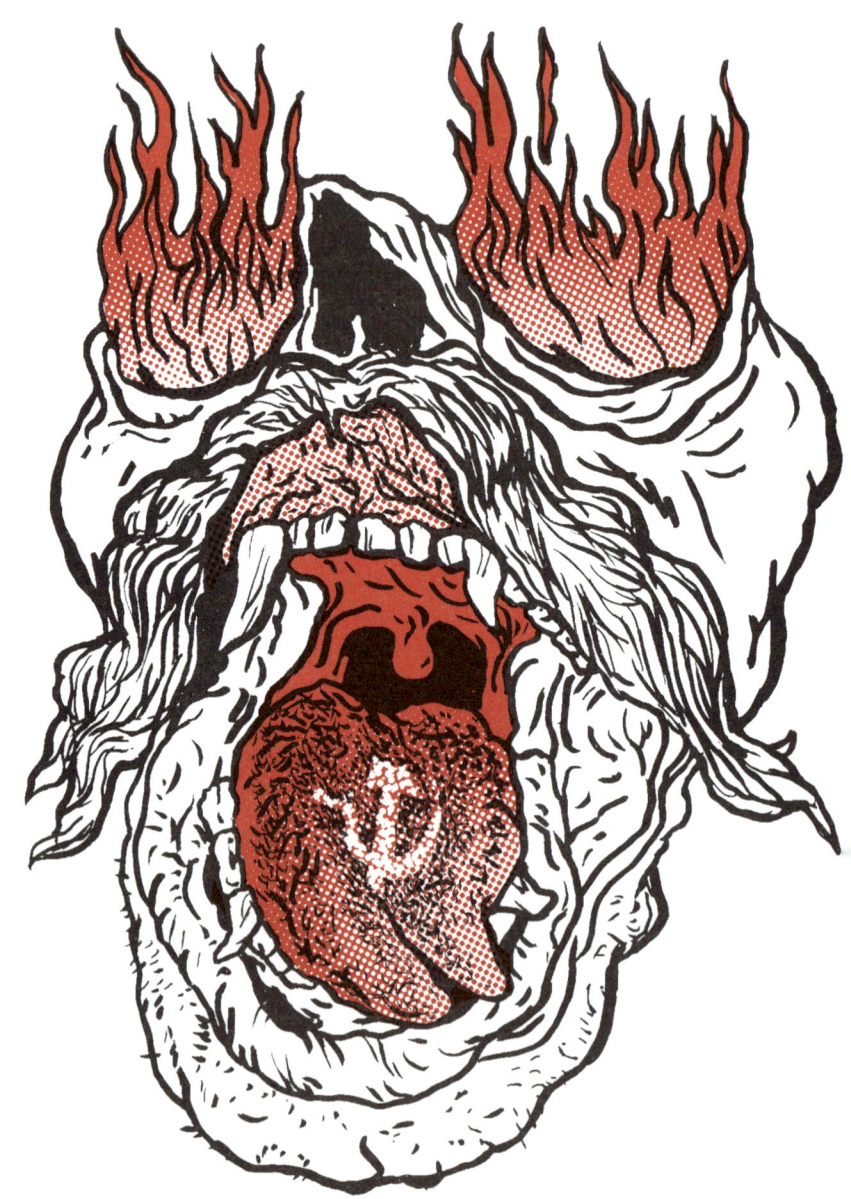

Estonia, Latvia, and Lithuania 1939–1956

- Gaslight: disinformation / accusing of fascism
- Invade: to protect
- Exterminate: genocide / settler colonialism

The Russian empire, now with the communism label, schemes to recolonize three Baltic states as part of a secret colonial deal with Nazi Germany [1]. Insisting it wants to protect itself, Moscow manufactures disinformation questioning the neutrality of Estonia, Latvia, and Lithuania. Then the empire bullies the nations into accepting military bases Moscow installs. The Kremlin uses them to invade in June 1940 based on false accusations of plotting and conspiring against Russia. Moscow installs puppet regimes, organizes sham elections, and uses the vote to justify the annexation. The colonization gets interrupted by a collapsed pact and a war with the Nazis, but after 1944 the Kremlin solidifies it [2]: ethnic cleansing in Estonia [3, 4, 5], Latvia [6], and Lithuania [7, 8] claims almost every fifth life through mass murder and deportation [9, 10]. In the following decades, Russification, identity erasure [11], and Russian settler colonialism pushes all three nations to the edge of annihilation [12]. Tens of thousands defend Baltic democracies for years by joining Forest Brothers, an anti-colo- nial guerilla resistance, but they eventually get outnumbered by Russian imperial troops by the mid-1950s [13, 14, 15]. The international community consents.

Exhibit 29

Romania
1940–1958

- Gaslight: disinformation
- Invade: to protect
- Exterminate: mass murder

The Russian empire, now under the communism label, schemes to partially colonize Romania following a secret colonial deal with Nazi Germany. Moscow manufactures disinformation claiming Romania is conspiring against Russia, vows to protect ethnic minorities, invades the country in June 1940, and annexes 15% of Romania with a population of over 3,700,000. The empire murders thousands in ethnic cleansing [1] and deports tens of thousands from annexed Northern Bukovyna and Moldova [2, 3]. In 1944, Moscow expands the occupation to all Romanian territory, bringing mass murder, looting, and rape to the country [4, 5]. With hundreds of thousands of Russian imperial troops on the ground, local pro-Russian communists claim victory in the 1946 elections, marred by widespread fraud, intimidation, and violence. The Kremlin mass exports Romanian resources to the metropole [6], including pillaging the country of uranium and leaving radioactive wastelands behind [7]. Thousands of Romanians join anti-colonial and anti-communist militant resistance, but they are outnumbered and crushed by the late 1950s [8, 9, 10, 11]. The international community consents.

Exhibit 30

Bulgaria
1944–1946

- Invade: to protect
- Exterminate: mass murder

The Russian empire, now under the communism label, invades Bulgaria in September 1944. Despite the country declaring neutrality several days earlier, Moscow insists on "liberation from fascism". Russian imperial troops assist a coup d'état by local Russia-backed communists and help to murder between 20,000 and 40,000 Bulgarians in the following months [1]. All opposition gets eradicated [2, 3]. A rigged 1946 referendum solidifies the grip of a satellite Moscow-controlled regime [4]. Thousands of Bulgarians join the fight for democratic Bulgaria in the anti-communist and anti-colonial Goryani rebellion — one of the earliest and longest-running of such kind in Eastern Europe. It is crushed by the early 1960s [5, 6]. The international community consents.

Exhibit 31

Hungary
1944–1956

- Gaslight: disinformation
- Invade: to protect
- Exterminate: mass murder

In 1944, the Russian empire, now under the communism label, invades Hungary to liberate it from fascism but maintains the occupation afterwards [1, 2]. The empire enslaves approximately 600,000 Hungarians for forced labor and deports them to Russia — every third of them dies [3, 4, 5]. In the 1945 parliamentary elections, pro-Russian communists win just 17% of the vote, but Moscow uses "salami tactics" to force a gradual communist takeover of the newly- founded Hungarian democracy and the installation of a satellite Moscow-controlled regime by 1949 [6, 7]. In 1956, Hungary tries to leave the Russian empire, and local students launch a popular pro-democracy uprising. Moscow manufactures disinformation, painting the resistance as a mob and foreign conspiracy [8]. It uses a facade collective security pact it enforces on Hungary and invades "to protect". Thousands of Hungarians are slaughtered by Russian imperial tanks, and the anti-colonial uprising is crushed [9, 10]. The international community consents.

Exhibit 32

Czechia and Slovakia 1945–1968

> Gaslight: disinformation
> Invade: to protect
> Exterminate: mass murder

In 1945, the Russian empire, now with the communism label, invades Czechoslovakia to liberate it from the Nazi German occupation. The country restores democracy, and by the end of 1945, most Russian troops go home, leaving behind somewhat positive public attitudes toward the Soviet Union. This contributes to the rising popularity of local communists, who take 40% of the votes in the 1946 election. However, by 1948, communist policies fail, and the popularity of pro-Russian forces starts dwindling. With Moscow's backing, local communists stage a coup and turn Czechoslovakia into a Russian satellite tyranny [1, 2, 3]. One of the leaders of the Czechoslovak democracy, Jan Masaryk, is found dead under mysterious circumstances [4]. In 1968, Czechs and Slovaks try to leave the Russian empire in a pro-democracy uprising. Moscow manufactures disinformation, painting them as extremists, criminals, and Western pawns [5, 6]. The empire enforces the "collective security pact" and invades "to protect". Outnumbered by a 250,000-strong Russian imperial troops, Czechs and Slovaks heroically resist but are defeated: 137 get killed under Russian tanks and 400 more in the mass murder that follows [7, 8, 9, 10, 11]. The international community consents.

Exhibit 33

Germany
1953

- Gaslight: disinformation
- Invade: to protect
- Exterminate: mass murder

After years of repressive and exploitative policies by a Moscow-installed satellite tyranny, the people of East Germany try to leave the Russian empire. Millions join a pro-democracy uprising in June 1953. The Kremlin and puppet German Democratic Republic manufacture disinformation, painting the protests as extremists, criminals, and Western pawns. Russian imperial tanks crush the uprising, killing dozens [1, 2, 3, 4, 5, 6]. The international community consents.

Exhibit 34

Afghanistan 1979–1989

- Gaslight: disinformation
- Invade: to protect
- Exterminate: failed, Russia is kicked out

There is little evidence of the Russian empire planning to absorb Afghanistan in the past, but Moscow has been keen on keeping it as a buffer from other colonial empires [1]. The Kremlin actively meddles with local politics, including two invasions in 1929 and 1930. By 1979, the Russian empire, now with the communism label, has spent decades putting in place a system of a political and military takeover, as well as economic exploitation of the country's resources [2]. As Afghanistan's political turbulence begins to threaten Russian influence, the Kremlin invades the country "to protect it from violence". Moscow is more preoccupied with Cold War scheming than the complexity of the on-the-ground situation and expects a quick victory within several days [3]. Things backfire as the invasion fuels anti-colonial resistance by Afghans. Russia is sucked into a decade-long war that kills between 500,000 and 2,000,000 people, or approximately 10% of the Afghan population, forcing millions to become refugees. Unpopular within the Russian empire and devastating to its international image, the invasion turbocharges the disintegration of the Russian communist regime in Moscow [4].

Exhibit 35

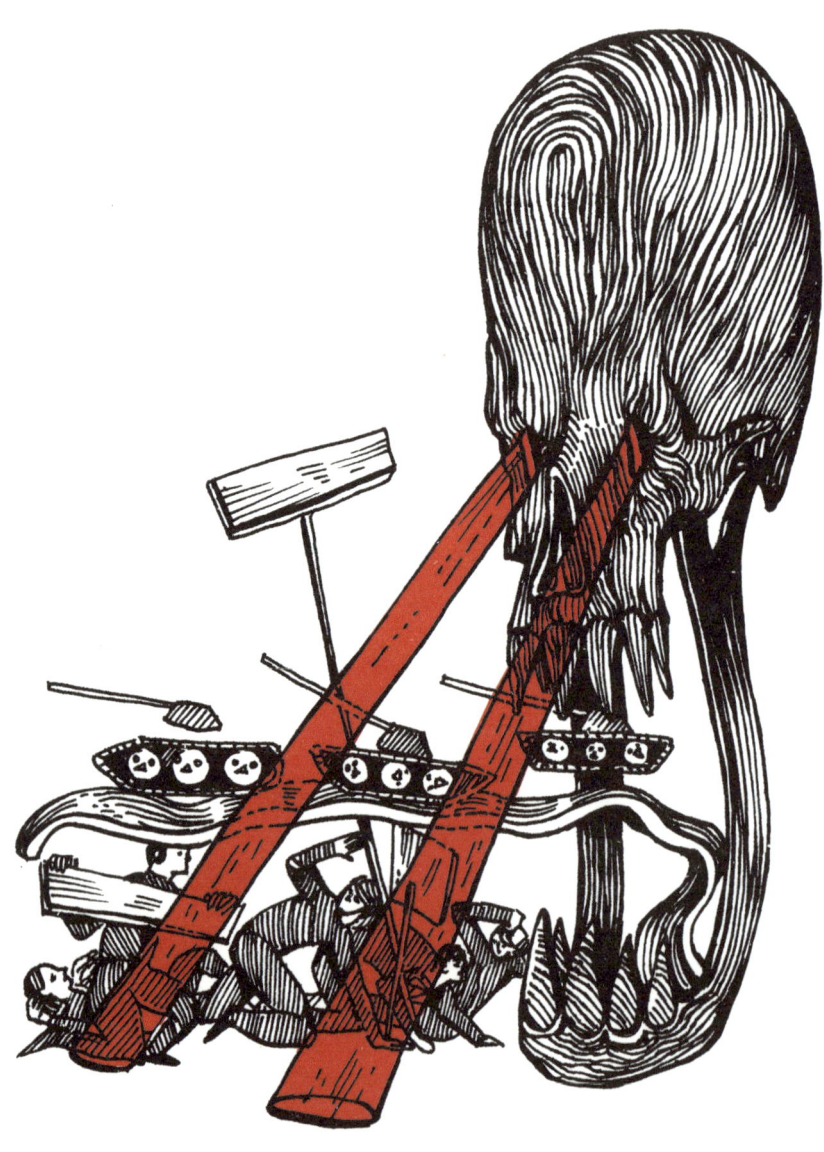

Qazaqstan
1986

- Gaslight: disinformation
- Invade: to protect
- Exterminate: failed, Russia is kicked out

After centuries of violent, exploitative colonial rule by Moscow, Qazaqstan revolts against Russian colonialism. The Jeltoqsan Uprising is a student-led, and pro-democracy movement. It is provoked by Moscow installing an outsider to rule the Qazaq colony. The Kremlin manufactures disinformation, branding the peaceful uprising as "hooligans" and "extremists", and dispatches kill squads against it: dozens of protesters are slaughtered. The crackdown backfires for the empire as Jeltoqsan turbocharges the independence push in Qazaqstan and inspires other anti-colonial movements within the collapsing empire [1, 2, 3, 4, 5, 6].

Exhibit 36

Sakartvelo (Georgia)
1989–1993

- Gaslight: fueling ethnic division
- Invade: to protect
- Exterminate: mass murder / territorial dismembering

After decades of despotic colonial rule, Sakartvelo decides to leave the Russian empire. Georgians (Kartvelians) launch a pro-democracy and anti-colonial uprising in Tbilisi. Moscow brands the peaceful protesters as "extremists" and dispatches tanks against them "to protect from disorder". Russian imperial troops use blunt weapons, shovels, and poisonous gas to disperse the crowd, killing 21 [1]. The crackdown backfires for Moscow: it turbocharges the full restoration of Georgian independence by 1991. Russian colonialism, now with the new "democratic Russia" label, punishes Sakartvelo by fueling ethnic strife. The Kremlin claims neutrality but keeps sending weapons and money to support breakaway regions [2]. Civil war kills thousands and fractures Sakartvelo [3], while Moscow retains a pro-Russian kleptocratic regime in the country [4, 5, 6].

Exhibit 37

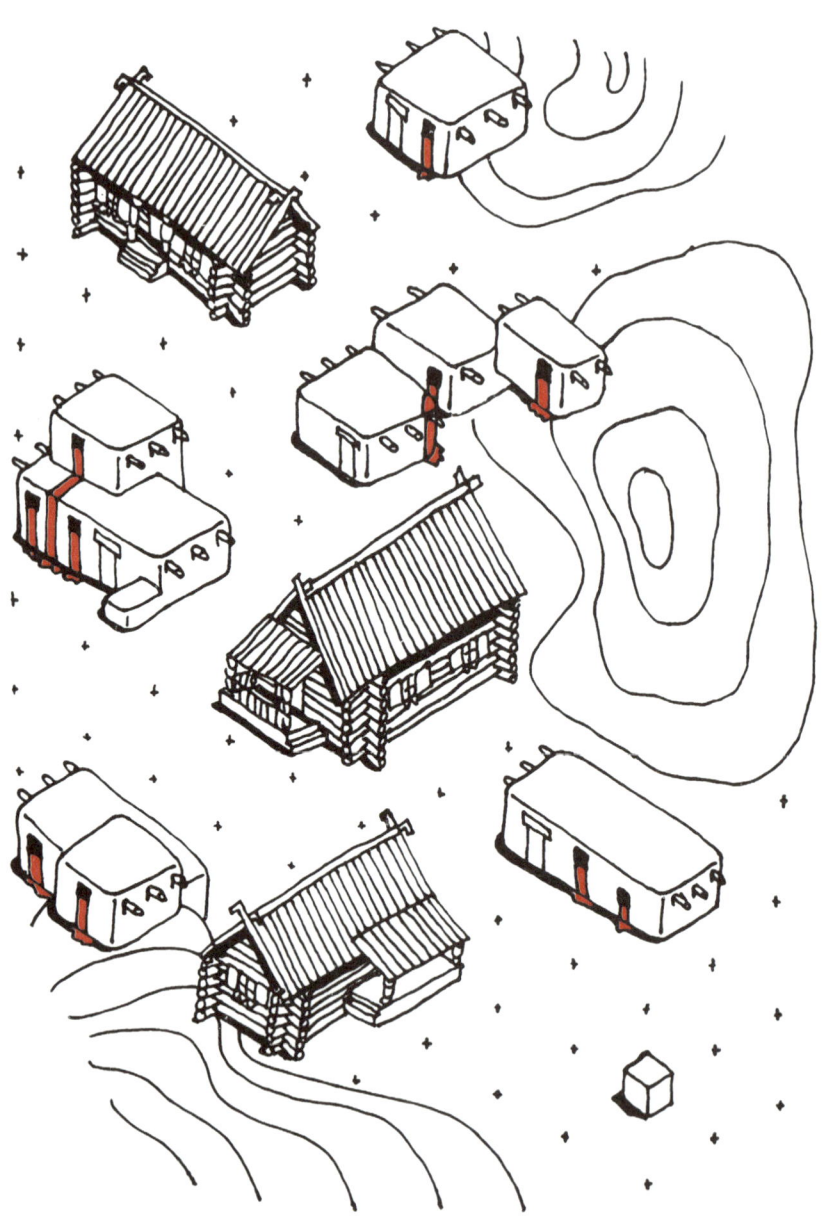

Azerbaijan
1989–1991

- Gaslight: fueling ethnic division
- Invade: to protect
- Exterminate: failed, Russia is kicked out

After decades of despotic colonial rule, Azerbaijanis decide to leave the Russian empire and rebel against the occupation with mass protests. Moscow doesn't want to lose an energy-rich colony and plans a crackdown on the burgeoning independence movement. In January 1990, the Kremlin uses local ethnic tensions as a far-fetched excuse to "protect Azerbaijanis from violence" and sends tanks against independence supporters in Baku, slaughtering an estimated 133 people [1, 2]. Instead of a quick triumph, the crackdown backfires for the empire: it turbocharges the full restoration of Azerbaijani independence by 1991. However, in the following years, the Russian empire, now with a "democratic Russia" label, exploits and fuels territorial and ethnic tensions within the country to retain hegemonic influence over Azerbaijan.

Exhibit 38

Lithuania
1990–1991

- Gaslight: fueling ethnic division
- Invade: to protect
- Exterminate: failed, Russia is kicked out

After decades of genocidal colonial occupation, Lithuania leaves the Russian empire and restores independence in March 1990. Moscow puts an economic blockade on the young democracy, manufactures disinformation to fuel ethnic strife [1], and sends tanks to "protect Russian speakers" [2]. Instead of a quick triumph, the crackdown backfires for the empire: it mobilizes Lithuanians of all ethnic and social backgrounds to defend their re-established democracy [3]. Russian colonial troops slaughter fifteen peaceful protesters but are demoralized by popular resistance and go home [4, 5, 6].

Exhibit 39

Latvia
1990–1991

- Gaslight: fueling ethnic division
- Invade: to protect
- Exterminate: failed, Russia is kicked out

After decades of genocidal colonial occupation, Latvia leaves the Russian empire and restores independence in May 1990. In January 1991, Moscow orchestrates bombings [1], stokes ethnic hatred, fuels fear and hysteria through disinformation, and dispatches kill squads to bully Latvians into submission [2]. Instead of a quick triumph, the crackdown backfires for the empire: it mobilizes Latvians to build street barricades and defend their newly restored democracy. Russian colonial squads slaughter six Latvian freedom fighters but are demoralized by popular resistance and go home [3, 4, 5, 6, 7].

Exhibit 40

Estonia
1991

- Invade: to protect
- Exterminate: failed, Russia is kicked out

After decades of genocidal colonial occupation, Estonia leaves the Russian empire. Following four years of peaceful resistance called the Signing Revolution, Estonians restore independence in August 1991. Moscow sends tanks to drag the country back into the empire. Instead of a quick triumph, the crackdown backfires for the empire: hundreds of thousands of Estonians mount street barricades, shield key state buildings with their bodies, and peacefully confront the colonial invaders. Russians are demoralized by popular resistance and go home [1, 2].

Exhibit 41

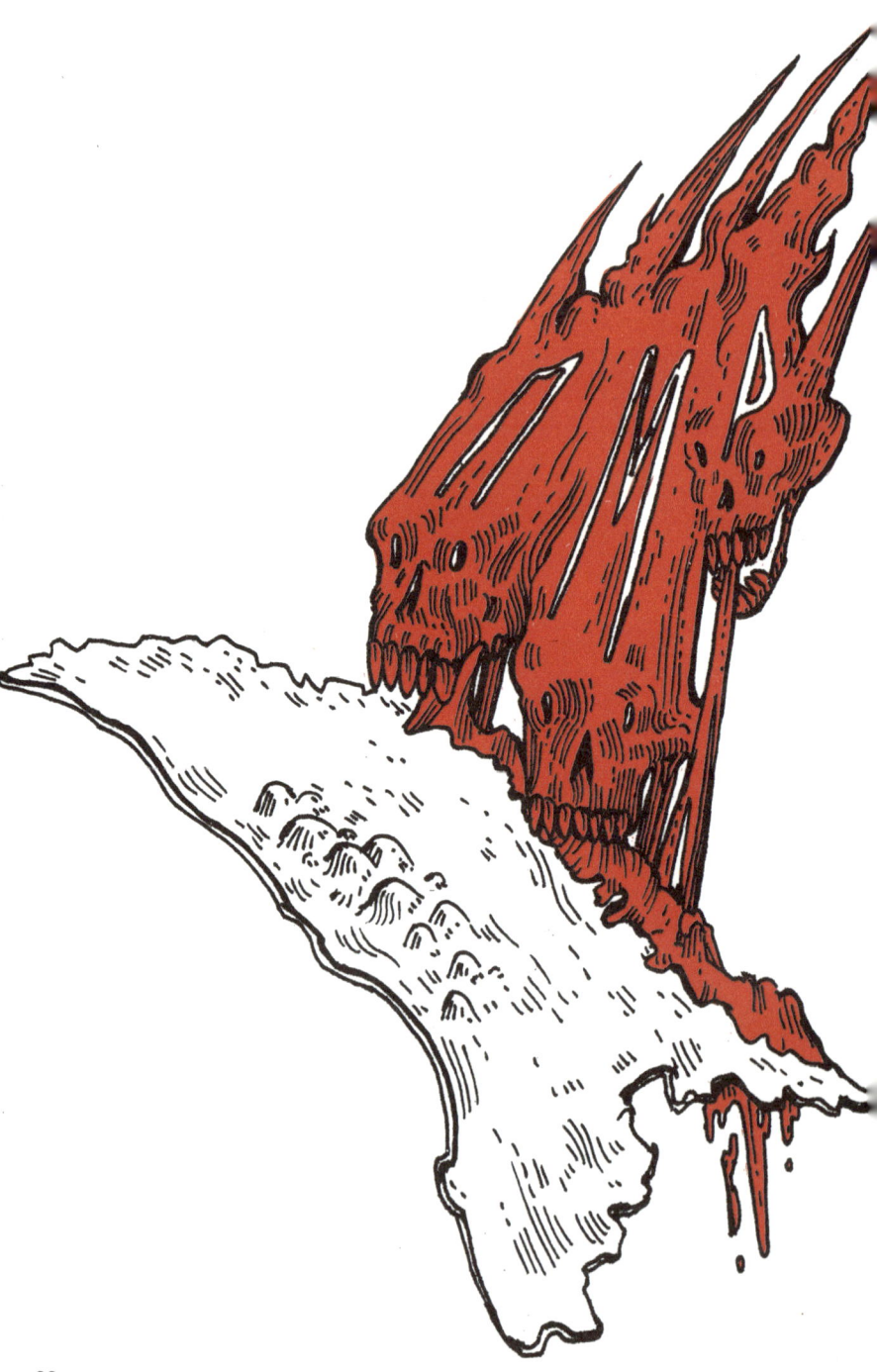

Moldova
1991

- Gaslight: fueling ethnic division
- Invade: to protect
- Exterminate: mass murder / territorial dismembering

Amid the collapse of the Soviet regime [1], Moldova leaves the Russian empire in 1991. Russian colonialism regroups, now with a "democratic Russia" label, and punishes Moldova by dismembering it. The Kremlin fuels ethnic strife that results in a civil war, killing hundreds. It uses the violence as a pretext to keep colonial troops on Moldovan territory "to protect" ethnic Russians and Russian speakers. The Kremlin de-facto takes over 10% of Moldovan territory by creating a puppet statelet of Transnistria [2]. Russians also fuel and finance separatist movements in the southern Moldovan region of Gagauzia [3]. Moldovans defend their democracy, but territorial dismemberment allows Russia to retain colonial influence over the country [4, 5, 6].

Exhibit 42

Tajikistan
1992–1997

- Invade: to protect
- Exterminate: mass murder

    Amid the collapse of the Soviet regime, Tajikistan leaves the Russian empire in 1991. The legacy of Russian colonial policies [1], which included identity erasure, manipulative rebordering, militarizing the country for imperial goals, and settler colonialism [2], contribute to the outbreak of civil war [3]. The Russian empire regroups, now with a "democratic Russia" label, and intervenes, citing the protection of ethnic Russians and Russian speakers [4, 5]. In reality, the Kremlin uses Russian troops stationed in the country to secure the victory of pro-Russian communists over pro-democratic and anti-colonial Islamist groups [6, 7]. The war ends in 1997, killing tens of thousands and displacing every fifth Tajik. At the same time, Moscow secures a loyal tyrannical regime for decades to come.

Exhibit 43

Ichkeria (Chechnya) 1991–2000

- Gaslight: disinformation / accusing of fascism
- Invade: to protect
- Exterminate: genocide

    Following centuries of genocidal colonial rule [1], the Chechens (Noxçiyçö) leave the Russian empire in 1991 and found The Chechen Republic of Ichkeria (Nóxçiyn Respublik Içkeri). The Russian empire regroups, now with a "democratic Russia" label, brands Chechens as extremists, and invades to "restore order and protect" in 1994. The first occupation collapses in 1996. Russian colonial troops return in 1999, buttressed by dehumanizing Putinist propaganda painting the Chechen anti-colonial struggle as "terrorist and nationalist" [2, 3, 4, 5]. Moscow wages another genocide of the Chechen people, razing local cities and villages to the ground, mass murdering civilians, and committing a wide range of grave war crimes [6, 7, 8]. As the international community looks the other way [9], an estimated 120,000 Chechens, or over 10% of the country's population, are slaughtered in both colonial conquests [10, 11]. The scale of violence helps Moscow to break the independence movements in Ichkeria and solidify colonial control [12, 13, 14].

Exhibit 44

Sakartvelo (Georgia)
2008

- Gaslight: stoking ethnic division / disinformation
- Invade: to protect
- Exterminate: ethnic cleansing / territorial dismembering

Sakartvelo kicks out a pro-Russian kleptocratic regime in the 2003 pro-democratic revolution [1, 2] and rapidly reforms away from Russian economic, cultural and political control. The Russian empire, now with the fascist Putinism label, decides to punish Georgian democracy by further dismembering it. Moscow manufactures disinformation about the "imminent genocide" of ethnic minorities within Sakartvelo, stages border provocations, and invades the country in August 2008 [3, 4]. As the international community looks away, the Kremlin ethnically cleanses the Abkhazia and South Ossetia regions of Georgia, along with killing 224 and displacing over 100,000 [5, 6, 7]. Russian colonial troops formally occupy 20% of Sakartvelo. In the following years, the Kremlin exploits territorial gains to strengthen political and economic influence over the country [8].

Exhibit 45

Ukraine
2014–2022

- Gaslight: stoking ethnic division / disinformation
- Invade: to protect
- Exterminate: territorial dismembering

Ukraine kicks out pro-Russian kleptocratic regimes in the 2004 and 2014 pro-democratic revolutions and rapidly reforms away from Russian economic, cultural, and political control [1, 2]. The Russian empire, now with the fascist Putinism label, decides to punish Ukrainian democracy by dismembering it. Moscow manufactures disinformation about ethnic strife, stokes political and cultural divides, and invades to "protect ethnic Russians and Russian speakers" [3]. The Kremlin sends covert troops [4, 5] to annex the Ukrainian region of Qırım-Crimea and sets up puppet statelets across eastern Ukraine. The Ukrainian society mobilizes for unprecedented pushback to defend democracy [6, 7, 8], but 7% of the Ukrainian territory ends up being occupied. Russia gradually slaughters over 14,000 Ukrainians in the creeping invasion [9] of the following eight years, and millions get displaced in a humanitarian catastrophe [10, 11, 12] as the West keeps pressuring Ukraine to settle for a status quo [13, 14]. This allows the Russian empire to walk away emboldened for new colonial conquests.

Exhibit 46

Syria
2015–2023

- Gaslight: disinformation
- Invade: to protect
- Exterminate: mass murder

Syrians launch a pro-democracy uprising and are about to overthrow a local tyrant. This endangers the future of Russian colonial troops in the region and a key Russian military base in Syria [1, 2, 3]. Moscow sends colonial troops to assist the pro-Russian tyranny under the pretense of stopping "imminent genocide". The Kremlin carpet bombs Syrian cities, targets civilians with chemical weapons, and commits a wide range of grave war crimes [4, 5, 6, 7]. Mass murder, assisted by Russian colonial troops, kills over 600,000 [8] and displaces more than 6,700,000 Syrians [9]. The international community consents and allows the Russian empire to walk away emboldened for new colonial conquests [10, 11, 12].

Exhibit 47

Ukraine
2022–TBC

After centuries of failed colonization attempts, the Russian empire [1], now with the fascist Putinism label [2, 3], opts out for a "final solution" for the Ukrainian multi-century resistance [4]. Moscow manufactures disinformation narratives about an impending "genocide" [5, 6] of ethnic and linguistic minorities, lies about non-existent plans of an invasion of Russia, and deploys dehumanizing language to deny the existence of the Ukrainian identity. In February 2022, the Kremlin uses formal recognition of its puppet statelets in eastern Ukraine as a front for a full-scale invasion to "protect" them. Russians resort to outright genocide [7, 8, 9, 10], razing Ukrainian cities and villages [11] to the ground, looting [12], deporting millions of Ukrainians [13, 14], and kidnapping Ukrainian kids for violent identity erasure. Moscow plans to take over Ukraine in several days, but the planned blitzkrieg fails, and Russian colonial troops face unprecedented resistance from Ukrainians defending their democracy.

1	Tannu-Tuva	1911–1944
2	Iran	1911–1946
3	Central Asia	1916–1934
4	Ukraine	1917–1953
5	Azerbaijan	1917–1920
6	Armenia	1917–1920
7	Sakartvelo (Georgia)	1917–1924
8	North Caucasus	1917–1945
9	Bashqortostan	1917–1921
10	Estonia	1917–1920
11	Qırım-Crimea	1917–1944
12	Don and Kuban'	1917–1920
13	Idel Ural	1917–1918
14	Belarus	1917–1921
15	Moldova	1917–1953
16	The Kalmyks-Xal'mgud	1917–1943
17	Buryad Mongolia	1917–1937
18	Latvia	1918–1920
19	Lithuania	1918–1920
20	Karelia-Karjala	1918–1922
21	The Tungus Republic	1918–1924
22	Sakha	1918–1927
23	Mongolia	1918–1941
24	The Khanty	1931–1933
25	The Dolgans	1932
26	The Nenets	1934–1943
27	Poland	1937–1947
28	Finland	1939–1940
29	Estonia, Latvia and Lithuania	1939–1956
30	Romania	1940–1958
31	Bulgaria	1944–1946
32	Hungary	1944–1956
33	Czechia and Slovakia	1945–1968
34	Germany	1953
35	Afghanistan	1979–1989
36	Qazaqstan	1986

37	Sakartvelo (Georgia)	1989–1993
38	Azerbaijan	1989–1991
39	Lithuania	1990–1991
40	Latvia	1990–1991
41	Estonia	1991
42	Moldova	1992
43	Tajikistan	1992–1997
44	Ichkeria (Chechnya)	1991–2000
45	Sakartvelo (Georgia)	2008
46	Ukraine	2014–2022
47	Syria	2015–2023
48	Ukraine	2022–TBC

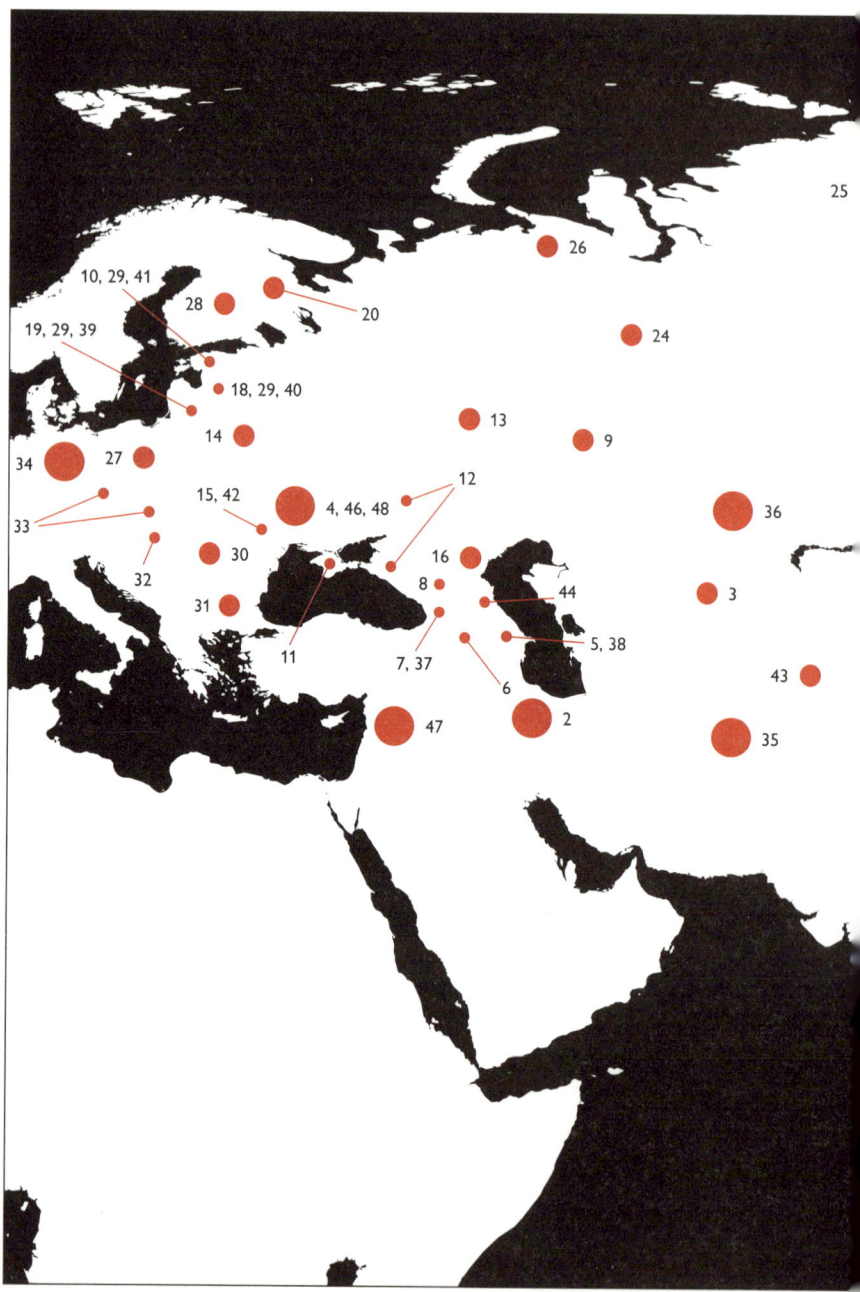

Mapping Russian colonial crimes
(1911–2023)

The following Ukrainian artists created the illustrations for this edition:

Sergiy Maidukov
Exhibit 19. Lithuania. 1918–1920
Exhibit 24. The Khanty. 1931–1933
Exhibit 35. Afghanistan. 1979–1989
Exhibit 37. Sakartvelo (Georgia). 1989–1993
Exhibit 47. Syria. 2015–2023
Exhibit 48. Ukraine. 2022–TBC

Alisa Gots
Exhibit 7. Sakartvelo (Georgia). 1917–1924
Exhibit 23. Mongolia. 1918–1941
Exhibit 27. Poland. 1937–1947
Exhibit 32. Hungary. 1944–1956
Exhibit 39. Lithuania. 1990–1991
Exhibit 41. Estonia. 1991
Exhibit 45. Sakartvelo (Georgia). 2008

Nikita Kravtsov
Exhibit 2. Iran. 1911–1946
Exhibit 4. Ukraine. 1917–1953
Exhibit 11. Qırım-Crimea. 1917–1944
Exhibit 22. Sakha. 1918–1927
Exhibit 28. Finland. 1939–1940
Exhibit 29. Estonia, Latvia, and Lithuania. 1939–1956
Exhibit 33. Czechia and Slovakia. 1945–1968

Nataliia Kozeko
Exhibit 1. Tannu-Tuva. 1911–1944
Exhibit 8. North Caucasus. 1917–1945
Exhibit 17. Buryad Mongolia. 1917–1937
Exhibit 20. Karelia-Karjala. 1918–1922
Exhibit 25. The Dolgans. 1932
Exhibit 34. Germany. 1953
Exhibit 46. Ukraine. 2014–2022

Danyl Shtangeev
Exhibit 6. Armenia. 1917–1920
Exhibit 15. Moldova. 1917–1953
Exhibit 18. Latvia. 1918–1920
Exhibit 21. The Tungus Republic. 1918–1924
Exhibit 26. The Nenets. 1934–1943
Exhibit 30. Romania. 1940–1958
Exhibit 44. Ichkeria (Chechnya). 1991–2000

Natasha Steshenko
Exhibit 3. Central Asia. 1916–1934
Exhibit 5. Azerbaijan. 1917–1920
Exhibit 9. Bashqortostan. 1917–1921
Exhibit 12. Don and Kuban'. 1917–1920
Exhibit 13. Idel Ural. 1917–1918
Exhibit 38. Azerbaijan. 1989–1991
Exhibit 43. Tajikistan. 1992–1997

Ave Libertatemaveamor
Exhibit 10. Estonia. 1917–1920
Exhibit 14. Belarus. 1917–1921
Exhibit 16. The Kalmyks-Xal'mgud. 1917–1943
Exhibit 31. Bulgaria. 1944–1946
Exhibit 36. Qazaqstan. 1986
Exhibit 40. Latvia. 1990–1991
Exhibit 42. Moldova. 1992

I was putting this book together during the darkest, most tragic days for my family, my people, and my country. It took an entire community to ensure that not only did I persevere, but also that this work would see the light of day amid genocide.

It all started with my husband Iaroslav, whose support made the difference between life and death. Everything I do and everything I am traces back to his love, care, and friendship. He was also the first sponsor of the Patreon community that launched this project back in early 2022.

This book is also dedicated to my family. To my mom, my dad, and my 93-year-old grandma, surviving and resisting Russian fascism just several kilometers away from the frontline. To my home village and the rest of the family enduring Russian occupation. To my dad-in-law, serving in the Ukrainian army and defending Ukraine. To my mom-in-law, surrounding me with support, love, and care while at the same time rebuilding her life anew as a refugee. And to so many of my relatives down the family tree who, under Russian colonialism, were murdered, kidnapped, deported, and disappeared. Survival runs in our blood.

I extend the same love, appreciation, and admiration to my extended family of friends. Especially my Ukrainian friends who, despite going through pain and trauma themselves, always have love, empathy, and support to share with others. You are the most unbreakable, kindest people I know.

A special shout-out goes to Rebecca, Shakina, and Musa for inspiring me to dare and take the first step toward this book. And to Botakoz — for ensuring I never waver and finish it.

I will remain eternally grateful to Anastasiia Leonova, Kateryna Nosko, Olya Balashova, and Sergiy Maidukov for being the first ones to sign up for the vision behind this guide. You are true trailblazers.

The manuscript for this guide would not have a fraction of the power it has now without the wartime Ukrainian art that has elevated the words. Alisa, Ave, Danyl, Nataliia, Natasha and Nikita — you've encapsulated these texts with real superpowers. My thanks also go to many friends and colleagues representing indigenous nations mentioned in the book. I am grateful for your help to ensure that your story and ancestral knowledge is represented fairly. This book exists in honor to centuries of the heroic resistance of your people to Russian colonialism.

This book is possible thanks to the kind donations of hundreds of people. I want to highlight exceptionally generous contributions by:
Akiko Asai,
Anastasia Kukharenko,
Betty,
Botakoz Kassymbekova,
Esther Angel,
Kateryna Halytska,
Leslie C,
Liubov Kukharenko,
Kinitaa Chandra,
Olha Ivanova,
Rebecca Harms,
Shakina Nayfack.

But also:
Alexander Engelhardt,
Amanda Rivers,

Anastasia Galadza,
Anastasiia Diudina,
Andrea Chalupa,
Andreas Nemlander,
ABK,
Angela Clyburn,
Anne-Isabelle Aebli,
Anssi Ruusuvuori,
Benjamin Rifkin,
Benjamin Wolf,
Cait Lotspeich,
Caroline Dunbar,
Chris H.,
Colin Spring,
Dana,
Daria Ilkina,
Dean Temple,
Dr. Nik Ford,
Dr. S. & Prof. Martha Trofimenko,
Frederic Denis,
Girard Mariano Lopez,
Hannes Grassegger,
Jānis Mucenieks,
Janusz & Joanna Palaczek,
Jesse Campbell,
Jo Crease,
Joni Kristian Pyysalo,
Joris Budénas,
Julia Guenther,
Juliana Loutsiouk,
Kate Higginson,
Katharina Schnoeder,
Katja Röcker,
Khrystyna Oros Ryan,
Kirsti Gabrielsen,
Klara & David,
Klara Woodson,
Lindsay,
Lucas Trost,
Maria Markevych & Vasyl Sywenky,
Maria Meier,
Martijn Kreek,
Maša Spalatin,
Michael Kania,
Michael Wirtz,
Monika Kollarova,
Natalie Poluha,
Paul Rowe,
Pavlo Melnyk,
Randy R. Potts,
Rob Martens,
Robin de Voh,
Roman Donchenko,
Sue Dymond,
Shelby Magid,
Shelley Jiang,
Ute Roericht,
Xeniya Kurochkina,
Yuliya Yurchuk,
Андрій Чернявський,
Вікторія Шолкова,
Данило Штангєєв,
Діана Цимбрикевич,
Дмитро Нечепуренко,
Ігор Крук,
Марина Лихошва,
Соломія Назаркевич,
Юлія Власкіна,
Юлія Корман,
Яна Троянська &
知也 古賀.

But also:
David Hume,
Kim Davalos,
Maggie,
Marco Malavasi,
Marina Hryhorash,
Martin Hübner,
Nina Smolnikova,
Sarah Ashton-Cirillo,
Stian Gjelseth,
Stuart Johnson,
Susanne Lundmark,
Thomas Garrett,
Victoria Pysmenna.

Above all, this guide exists in honor of my fellow Ukrainians defending their homes and fighting for the right to be. Their hardship paves the way for a better world for all of us. Their voices are impossible to silence. Their stories deserve to be heard.

 All the sources can be found at this QR code.

Introduction

1. Volya Hub. "What Is Colonialism, and Why It Concerns Russian Neighbors?" *YouTube*, 21 December 2022.
2. Volya Hub. "Why Russia is a Colonial Empire?" *YouTube*, 26 January 2023.
3. Eristavi, Maksym (maksymeristavi). "Mother of All Russian Colonialism Threads," thread. 20 February 2022, 10:02 a.m. Twitter thread.
4. Kassymbekova, Botakoz, and Marat Erica. "Time to Question Russia's Imperial Innocence." *PONARS Eurasia Policy Memo*, no. 771, 27 April 2022.
5. ТУЧА (TUCHA). "Russia Is a Terrorist State." *YouTube*, 24 August 2022.

Exhibit 1. Tannu-Tuva. 1911–1944

1. Leonov, Nikolai. *Tannu-Tuva: the Country of the Blue River.* [Rus.] Publishing House of the Politktorzhan Society, 1927.
2. Mollerov, Nikolai. "Soviet Diplomats and Comintern Representatives in People's Republic of Tuva in the 1920s." [Rus.] *Novye Issledovaniya Tuvy–The New Research of Tuva*, no. 3 (31), 2016.
3. Grebneva, V. *Geography of Tuva.* [Rus.] Kyzyl, 1968.
4. Otroshchenko, Ivanna. "Tuva's Accession to the USSR: Alternative Opinions." [Rus.] *Novye Issledovaniya Tuvy–The New Research of Tuva*, no. 4, 2017.
5. Mongush, Mergen. "The Annexation of Tannu-Tuva and the Formation of the Tuvinskaya ASSR." [Rus.] *Nationalities Papers*, no. 2, 1993.

Exhibit 2. Iran. 1911–1946

1. Browne, Edward Granville. *Letters from Tabriz: the Russian Suppression of the Iranian Constitutional Movement.* Mage Publishers, 2008.
2. Andreeva, Elena, and Morteza Nouraei. "Russian Settlements in Iran in the Early Twentieth Century: Initial Phase of Colonization." *Iranian Studies*, no. 3, 2013.
3. Chaqueri, Cosroe. *The Soviet Socialist Republic of Iran, 1920–21: Birth of the Trauma.* Pittsburgh University Press, 1994.
4. Faramarz, Davar. "For Iranians, Putin's Invasion of Ukraine Revives a Historic Fear." *Iran Wire*, 25 February 2022.
5. The Cold War. "Post-WWII Iran — British and Soviet Occupation and the Revolution — COLD WAR." *YouTube*, 27 July 2019.
6. Lenczowski, George. *Russia and the West in Iran: A Study in Big Power Rivalry, 1918–1948.* Cornell University Press, 1949.

Exhibit 3. Central Asia. 1916–1934

1. Marat, Erica. "Introduction: 30 Years of Central Asian Studies — the Best Is Yet to Come." *Central Asian Survey*, vol. 40, no. 4, 2021.
2. Kassymbekova, Botakoz; Chokobaeva, Aminat. "On Writing Soviet History of Central Asia: Frameworks, Challenges, Prospects." *Central Asian Survey*, vol. 40, no. 4, 2021.
3. Azmi, M. Raziullah. "Russian Expansion in Central Asia and the Afghan Question (1865–85)." *Pakistan Horizon*, vol. 37, no. 3, 1984.
4. Northrop, Douglas. *Veiled Empire: Gender and Power in Stalinist Central Asia.* Cornell University Press, 2003.
5. "Communist Dictatorship in Uzbekistan (1918–1991)." *Uzbekistan | Communist Crimes.*
6. Penati, Beatrice. "The Reconquest of East Bukhara: The Struggle against the Basmachi As a Prelude to Sovietization." *Central Asian Survey*, vol. 26, no. 4, 2007.
7. Martha B. Olcott. "The Basmachi or Freemen's Revolt in Turkestan 1918–24." *Soviet Studies*, vol. 33, no. 3, 1981.
8. Florin, Moritz. "Beyond Colonialism? : Agency, Power, and the Making of Soviet Central Asia." *Kritika: Explorations in Russian and Eurasian History*, vol. 18, no. 4, 2017.
9. Chokobaeva, Aminat. "Frontiers of Violence: State and Conflict in Semirechye, 1850–1938." *The Australian National University*, 2017.
10. Ellis C. H. "The New Colonialism." *Journal of The Royal Central Asian Society*, vol. 49, no. 3–4, 1962.
11. Morrison, Alexander. "Settler Bolsheviks in the Soviet 'Eastern'." *Cinematic Settlers: The Settler Colonial World in Film.* Routledge, New York, 2020.
12. Rywkin, Michael. "Central Asia and the Price of Sovietization." *Problems of Communism*, vol. 8, no. 1, 1964.

Sources

Exhibit 4. Ukraine. 1917–1953
1. Plokhy, Serhii. *Unmaking Imperial Russia: Mykhailo Hrushevsky and the Writing of Ukrainian History.* University of Toronto Press, 2005.
2. Kvit, Serhiy. "One Hundred Years of the Ukrainian Liberation Struggle." *Kyiv-Mohyla Humanities Journal,* no. 4, 2017.
3. "Communist Dictatorship in Ukraine. The Soviet Occupation (1920–1991)." *Ukraine | Communist Crimes.*
4. Shtohryn, Iryna. "90 Years since the Beginning of Mass Rozkurkulennia: How the Communist Party Destroyed the Peasant Owner." [Ukr.] *Radio Svoboda,* 30 January 2020.
5. "About the Project." *Deportations. Visual Memory.*
6. "Home." *National Museum of the Holodomor-Genocide.*
7. Gliński, Mikołaj. "The Executed Renaissance: The Book That Saved Ukrainian Literature from Soviet Oblivion." *Culture.Pl,* 3 March 2022.
8. Zhygun, Snizhana. "Why Is the History of Ukrainian Literature Silent about the Women Writers of the Second and Third Decades of the 20th Century?" *Transilvania,* no. 11–12, 2021.
9. Snyder, Timothy. *Sketches from a Secret War: A Polish Artist's Mission to Liberate Soviet Ukraine.* Yale University Press, 2007.
10. Snyder, Timothy. *Bloodlands: Europe between Hitler and Stalin.* Basic Books (AZ), 2010.

Exhibit 5. Azerbaijan. 1917–1920
1. Balayev, Aydin. "March 1918: A Defining Moment for Azerbaijan." *ADA Biweekly,* vol. 1, no. 18, 2008.
2. "Communist Dictatorship in Azerbaijan. The Soviet Occupation (1920–1991)." *Azerbaijan | Communist Crimes.*
3. Hasanli, Jamil. *The Sovietization of Azerbaijan: The South Caucasus in the Triangle of Russia, Turkey, and Iran, 1920–1922.* University of Utah Press, 2017.

Exhibit 6. Armenia. 1917–1920
1. Ketsemanian, "Varak. Records, Discourses and Memories: Narrating the First Republic." *EVN Report,* 25 May 2018.
2. "Communist Dictatorship in Armenia. The Soviet Occupation (1921–1991)." *Armenia | Communist Crimes.*

Exhibit 7. Sakartvelo (Georgia). 1917–1924
1. Berdy, Michele A. "The Experiment: Georgia's Forgotten Revolution 1918–1921." *The Moscow Times,* 1 February 2020.
2. "Republic 100." *Civil.ge.*
3. Shame Movement. "100 years in 100 seconds." *YouTube,* 23 February 2021.
4. Chkadua, Giorgi. "The August 1924 Uprising: Plan, Outcome, Interpretation. Russia's Expansion in the Caucasus and Georgia." *Georgian Foundation for Strategic and International Studies.*
5. *Soviet Past Research Laboratory.*
6. "February 25, 1921 – Heroic Georgians Who Fought against Russia's Red Army." *Georgian Journal,* 25 February 2016.
7. "National Archives Online Display Marks Soviet Invasion Centenary." *Agenda.ge,* 25 February 2021.

Exhibit 8. North Caucasus. 1917–1945
1. Çelikpala, Mitat. *Search for a Common North Caucasian Identity: The Mountaineers' Attempts for Survival and Unity in Response to the Russian Rule.* Bilkent Universitesi, 2002.
2. Pohl, Jonathan Otto. "Scourging the Caucasus: The Soviet Deportation of the Karachais, Chechens, Ingush, and Balkars in 1943–1944." *Forum of EthnoGeoPolitics,* vol. 3, no. 1, 2015.
3. Kassymbekova, Botakoz. "Exotic Bodies in Soviet Culture: The Caucasus, Empire, and Revolutionary Old Age." *The Russian Review,* vol. 19, no. 3, 1960.
4. Sultanov, Akhmed, Yelkhoyev, Lecha, Bigg, Claire. "'There Was No Water, No Food' — Chechens Remember Horror of 1944 Deportations." *Radio Liberty,* 22 February 2014.
5. Nadskakuła, Olga. "The Genocide of Chechens in the Context of Russian-Chechen Conflict — A Historical Outline." *The Person and the Challenges,* vol. 3, no. 2, 2013.

Exhibit 9. Bashqortostan. 1917–1921
1. Musagalieva, Arajlym Sabytovna, and Musabekova, Rosa Madenietovna. "The Kazakh Intelligentsia in the Struggle with Soviet power: New Sources and Interpretations." [Rus.] *Young*

Scientist — Molodoy Uchenyi, no. 17, 2016.
2. Togan, Ahmed Zeki Velidi, and Hasan B. Paksoy. *Memoirs: National Existence and Cultural Struggles of Turkistan and Other Muslim Eastern Turks.* 2012.
3. Kulsharipov M.M. *Bashkir National Movement (1917–1921).* [Rus.] KITAP, 2000.
4. Taymasov, R. S. "The Baymak Execution of 1918." [Rus.] *Military History of the Bashkirs: An Encyclopedia,* 1 October 2019.
5. Musagalieva, Araylym Sabitovna. "Zaki Valida and the National Intelligentsia of Kazakhstan." [Rus.] *Bulletin of the Academy of Sciences of the Republic of Bashkortostan,* vol. 15, no. 1, 2010.

Exhibit 10. Estonia. 1917–1920
1. Vahtla, Aili (ed.). "Part 1: Estonian Independence Proclaimed in Pärnu on Feb. 23." *ERR,* 3 February 2018.
2. Vahtla, Aili (ed.). "Part 3: First Blood Spilled for Sovereign Estonia on Feb. 25." *ERR,* 17 February 2018.
3. Eastory. "Estonian War of Independence Animated." *YouTube.* 21 January 2018.
4. Whyte, Andrew (ed.). "Local Governments Mark 100th Anniversary of Constituent Assembly Elections." *ERR,* 5 April 2019.
5. Annus, Epp. *Soviet Postcolonial Studies: A View from the Western Borderlands.* Routledge, 2017.

Exhibit 11. Qırım-Crimea. 1917–1944
1. МІНКУЛЬТ (MINCULT). "We Are Crimean Tatars." [Qir., Eng sub.] *YouTube,* 18 May 2016.
2. "About Crimean Tatars." *Ctrcenter.*
3. "Crimean Tatar People Mourned for Its Great Son Noman Chelebicihan." *Islam in Ukraine,* 24 February 2010.
4. Chehovych, V. A. "Soviet Socialist Republic of Tavrida." *Judicial encyclopedia. National Academy of Sciences of Ukraine, The Korestskyi Institute of State and Law,* Publishing house "Ukrainian Encyclopedia" named after M. P. Bazhana, 1998–2004.
5. Hromenko, Serhiy. *The Forgotten Victory: Peter Bolbochan's Crimean Operation of 1918.* [Ukr.] Ukrainian Institute of National Remembrance, 2018.
6. Shurkhalo, Dmytro. "Crimean Autonomy: How It Was Created in 1921 and Recreated in 1991." [Ukr.] *Radio Svoboda,* 7 November 2021.
7. Crimean Tatars in English. "Deportation of Chechens and Ingushes." *YouTube.* 16 April 2018.
8. Hromadske. "Deported Crimean Tatar Recalls the Tragedy of 1944." [Rus., Eng. sub.] *YouTube.* 18 May 2016.
9. UATV English. "Still in the Shadow of Genocide, Crimean Tatars Mourn 1944 Deportations." *YouTube,* 18 May 2018.
10. Matviychuk, Mykola. "Deportation of the Crimean Tatar People. History of Genocide." *Suspilne Crimea,* 18 May 2022.
11. Voloshyna, Larysa. "Who and When Lived in Crimea? We Debunk Myths." [Ukr.] *Ukrainska Pravda,* 09 August 2021.
12. Sviezhentsev, Maksym; Kisly, Martin-Oleksandr. "Race in Time and Space: Racial Politics Towards Crimean Tatars in Exile, Through and After Return (1944–1991)." *Krytyka,* June 2021.

Exhibit 12. Don and Kuban'. 1917–1920
1. Matychak, Tetyana. "Why Are Cossacks Key to Understanding the Ukrainian Nation?" *UkraineWorld,* 13 March 2019.
2. Plokhy, Serhii. *The Cossack Myth: History and Nationhood in the Age of Empires.* Cambridge University Press, 2012.
3. Pyvovarov, Serhii; Spirin, Yevhen. "104 Years Ago Kuban People's Republic Declared Its Independence from Russia and for Several Times Tried to Unite with Ukraine. As a Result, Bolsheviks Captured Everyone — Here's Its Story." *Babel,* 16 February 2022.
4. Prykhodko, M. M. "Interstate Alliance of the Ukrainian State of Hetman Skoropadskyi and the All-Great Army of the Don Ataman Krasnov." *Gilea: Scientific Bulletin,* no. 80, 2014.
5. Popok, Andrii Andrijovych. "Malynovyi Klyn." [Ukr.] *Encyclopedia of the History of Ukraine,* 2009.
6. Babich, Irina Leonidovna. "Kubans and Caucasians: Together and Apart in European Emigration (1919–1930s)." *Scientific Thought of the Caucasus,* no. 1 (69), 2012.
7. Bilyj, Dmytro Dmytrovych. "Kuban People's Republic, Independent Kuban People's Republic, Kuban Territory" [Ukr.] *Encyclopedia of the History of Ukraine,* 2008.

8. Bilyj, Dmytro Dmytrovych. *Ukrainians of the Kuban in 1792–1921: The Evolution of Social Identities.* [Ukr.] Eastern Publishing House, 2009.
9. Heller, Mikhail, Aleksandr Nekrich. *Utopia in Power: The History of the Soviet Union from 1917 to the Present.* Summit Books, 1986.

Exhibit 13. Idel Ural. 1917–1918

1. Garifullin, Ilnar. "Born by the Revolution. The Tatar Parliament Turned 100 Years Old." [Rus.] *Idel Real,* 30 November 2017.
2. Devlet, Nadir. "Millät Mäclese (36)." [Tat.] *Azalliq Radiosi,* 12 September 2011.
3. "Free Idel-Ural: Civil Movement."
4. Garifullin, Ilnar. "Kharbi Shuro — the Interrupted History of the Tatar National Army. Part II. Rise and Fall of the Military Council." [Rus.] *Idel Real,* 10 January 2018.
5. Garifullin, Ilnar. "Indecisiveness and Slowness: Why Was It Impossible to Build the Idel-Ural Republic." [Rus.] *Idel Real,* 04 August 2018.
6. Bashkirica. "Bashkir tragedy." [Rus.] *YouTube,* 30 June 2011.

Exhibit 14. Belarus. 1917–1921

1. Sviadomi. "Russification of Belarus." [Bel, Rus, Eng.] *YouTube,* 11 March 2023.
2. Marin, Anaïs. "Belarusian Nationalism in the 2010s: A Case of Anti-Colonialism? Origins, Features and Outcomes of Ongoing 'Soft Belarusianisation'." *Journal of Belarusian Studies,* vol. 9, no. 1, 2020.
3. "25 Questions and Answers from the History of the BPR." [Bel.] *Euroradio,* 25 March 2017.
4. Pechanko, Siamen. "Women Who Linked Their Fate with BPR." [Bel.] *Salidarnasts,* 08 March 2018.
5. Michaluk, Dorota. *The Belarusian People's Republic 1918–1920: At the Foundation of Belarusian Statehood.* [Pół.] Wydawnictwo Naukowe Uniwersytetu Mikołaja Kopernika, 2010.
6. Krapivin, Siarhey. "Grandma with a Red Wagon in Front of 'Europe'." [Rus.] *Naviny.by,* 24 March 2009.
7. Lebedzeva, Valiantsina. "BPR–UPR: The First Experience of State Relations (Spring 1918)." [Bel.] *Local history site of Gomel and Gomel Oblast,* 16 December 2009.

8. BELSAT HISTORY. "Territorial Claims Grew into Friendship." [Bel.] *YouTube,* 2 May 2022.
9. Lahvinets, Ales; Chulitskaya, Tatsiana (eds.). *Belarus and Belarusians Among Neighbors: Historical Stereotypes and Political Constructs.* [Bel.] Uczelnia Łazarskiego, 2013.
10. Radio Liberty. "The Slutsk Military Uprising. Explained with Toy Soldiers." *YouTube,* 24 November 2018.
11. "Communist Dictatorship in Belarus (1918–1991)." *Belarus | Communist Crimes.*
12. Lewis, Simon. "The 'Partisan Republic': Colonial Myths and Memory Wars in Belarus." *War and Memory in Russia, Ukraine and Belarus,* Palgrave Macmillan, 2017.

Exhibit 15. Moldova. 1917–53

1. Ungureanu, Constantin. "Population of Bukovina and Bessarabia under Imperial Domination (1775/1812 – 1918)." [Rom.] *Archiva Moldaviae,* no. 5, 2013.
2. Dumitru, Diana; Negura, Petru (eds.). "Moldova: A Borderland's Fluid History." *Online Journal of the Center for Governance and Culture in Europe, University of St. Gallen,* no. 15–16, 2014.
3. History Matters. "Why Does Moldova Exist? (Short Animated Documentary)." *YouTube,* 24 June 2020.
4. Chehovych V. A. "Moldovan Autonomous Soviet Socialist Republic." [Ukr.] *Judicial encyclopedia.*
5. "Communist Occupation and Dictatorship in Moldova (1918–1941; 1944–1991)." *Moldova | Communist Crimes.*
6. Erizanu, Paula. "70 Years On, a New Animation Revisits the Painful History of Stalin's Deportation of Moldovans." *The Calvert Journal,* 30 September 2019.

Exhibit 16. The Kalmyks-Xaľmgud 1917–1943

1. Mueggenberg, Brent. *The Cossack Struggle Against Communism, 1917–1945.* McFarland, 2019.
2. Badmaeva, Ekaterina. "The Fight Against Mass Famine and Its Consequences in Kalmykia 1921–1924." [Rus.] *Stavropol State University,* Elista, 2001.
3. Badmaeva, Ekaterina, and Omakaeva, Ellara.

"Famine in Kalmykia (1932–1933)." *European Proceedings of Social and Behavioural Sciences,* European Publisher, 2021.

4. Guchinova, Elza-Bair Matsakovna. "Everyone Has Their Own Siberia. Two Stories about the Deportation of the Kalmyks (Interviews with S.M. Ivanov and S.E. Naranova)." [Rus.] *Oriental Studies,* no. 3 (43), 2019.

5. "'Punished Peoples' of the Soviet Union: The Continuing Legacy of Stalin's Deportations." *Human Rights Watch,* vol. 1245, 1991.

6. Biurchiev, Badma. "Kalmykia's Long Goodbye." *OpenDemocracy,* 22 December 2016.

7. "Kalmykia: Demographics." *Wikipedia.*

Exhibit 17. Buryad Mongolia. 1917–1937

1. Khamutaev, Vladimir A. *Annexation of Buryatia to Russia: History, Law, Politics.* ARAMNG, 2012.

2. Ratcliffe, Jonathan. "Becoming-Geser, Becoming-Buryat: Oral Epic and the Politics of Navigating Four Identity Crises." *Australian National University,* 2019.

3. Aronova, Marina. "How the Only Theocracy in Russia Arose in Response to Mobilization. And What Came of It." [Rus.] *Sibir Realii,* 12 September 2022.

4. Babakov, *Victor Valerievich. Burnatsky-Burnardum: The First Experience of Nation-State Building in Buryatia.* [Rus.] 1997.

5. James Minahan. *Encyclopedia of the Stateless Nations: Ethnic and National Groups Around the World, Vol. 4: S–Z.* Greenwood, 2002.

6. Free Nations League. "Rajana Dugar-DePonte about Three Waves of the Buryat National Movement." *YouTube,* 22 July 2022.

Exhibit 18. Latvia. 1918–1920

1. Šiliņš, Jānis. "Latvia at a Crossroads: November 1917." *LSM.lv,* 2 November 2017.

2. Ķibilds, Mārtiņš. Latvia's Independence Day — But a Single Step in a Long Journey. *LSM.lv,* 18 November 2018.

3. "Home." *Museum of the Occupation of Latvia.*

4. Šiliņš, Jānis. "The Republic on the Sea: The 1919 Coup that Exiled the Latvian Government to a Steamboat." *LSM.lv,* 18 April 2019.

5. Šiliņš, Jānis. "100 Years Since Rīga Was Freed from Communist Rule." *LSM.lv,* 23 May 2019.

6. Ministry of Foreign Affairs of the Republic of Latvia. "Latvia-Russia Peace Treaty 100." *Facebook,* 11 August 2020.

7. History Matters. "The Molotov-Ribbentrop Pact — History Matters (Short Animated Documentary)." *YouTube,* 30 April 2019.

Exhibit 19. Lithuania. 1918–1920

1. Žemaitis, Augustinas. "The Rule of Russian Empire in Lithuania (1795–1918)." *TrueLithuania.com.*

2. Žemaitis, Augustinas. "Ethnic Relations in Lithuania During Russian Empire (1795–1918)." *TrueLithuania.com.*

3. Waters, Michael. "The 19th-Century Lithuanians Who Smuggled Books to Save Their Language." *Atlas Obscura,* 19 July 2017.

4. Snyder, Timothy. *The Reconstruction of Nations: Poland, Ukraine, Lithuania, Belarus, 1569–1999.* Yale University Press, 2002.

5. Annus, Epp. "The Problem of Soviet Colonialism in the Baltics." *Journal of Baltic Studies,* vol. 43, no. 1, 2012.

6. Misiūnas, Virginijus. "Lithuania Independence War 1918–1923." *YouTube,* 17 February 2018.

Exhibit 20. Karelia-Karjala. 1918–1922

1. Riitta, Raatikainen. "Karelia and Karelian People in Nordic Expeditioners' Photographs from the Late 19th Century." [Rus.] *Almanac of Northern European and Baltic Studies,* no. 5, 2020.

2. Malinen, Ismo. "Conflicts in Karelia. The Military Expedition of 1921–1922 to Karelia Was Documented by Erkki Räikkönen." *Finnish Heritage Agency.*

3. "East Karelian Uprising 1921–1922." *Heninen.net.*

4. Horváth, Csaba. "Ethnogeographic Metamorphosis of East Karelia during the 20th Century." *Délkelet Európa – South-East Europe. International Relations Quarterly,* vol. 1, no. 2, 2010.

5. Kurs, Ott. "Indigenous Finnic Population of NW Russia." *GeoJournal,* vol. 34, no. 4, 1994.

6. Kostiainen, Auvo. "Genocide in Soviet Karelia: Stalin's Terror and the Finns of Soviet Karelia." *Scandinavian Journal of History,* vol. 21, no. 4, 1996.

7. Sevander, Mayme. *They Took My Father: Finnish*

Americans in Stalin's Russia. University of Minnesota Press, 1992.

Exhibit 21. The Tungus Republic. 1918–1924
1. Pronyakin, Konstantin. "The Okhotsk Region Almost Became Tungusia." [Rus.] *Khabarovsk Express,* no. 42, 14 October 2009.
2. Pesterev Vladimir Ilyich. *Historical Miniatures about Yakutia.* Bichik, Yakutsk, 1993.
3. Shirokogoroff, S. M. "Tungus Literary Language." *Asian Folklore Studies,* vol. 50, no. 1, 1991.

Exhibit 22. Sakha. 1918–1927
1. Hill, Fiona, and Clifford G. Gaddy. *The Siberian Curse: How Communist Planners Left Russia out in the Cold.* Brookings Institution Press, 2003.
2. Korobeinikov, Aleksandr, and Egor Antonov. "Toward a Postimperial Order? : The Sakha Intellectuals and the Revolutionary Transformations in Late Imperial Russia, 1905–1917." *Sibirica,* vol. 20, no. 2, 2021.
3. Forsyth, James. *A History of the Peoples of Siberia: Russia's North Asian Colony 1581–1990.* Cambridge University Press, 1994.
4. Vasilyeva, Tatyana. "Unknown Report by Mikhail Kornilov." [Rus.] *Sakha Open World,* November 2021.
5. Sidorova, Evgeniia, and Roberta Rice. "Being Indigenous in an Unlikely Place: Self-determination in the Yakut Autonomous Soviet Socialist Republic (1920–1991)." *The International Indigenous Policy Journal,* vol. 11, no. 3, 2020.
6. Karpukhina, Yekaterina; Coalson, Robert. "Stalin's Great Terror: Sakha's Mountain of Tin and Bones." *Radio Liberty,* 4 October 2017.
7. Tichotsky, John. *Russia's Diamond Colony: The Republic of Sakha.* Routledge, 2014.

Exhibit 23. Mongolia. 1918–1941
1. China Uncensored. "How China Colonized Half of Mongolia." *YouTube,* 02 March 2020.
2. Elleman, Bruce A. "Secret Sino-Soviet Negotiations on Outer Mongolia, 1918–1925." *Pacific Affairs,* vol. 66, no. 4, 1993.
3. Barany, Zoltan. "Soviet Takeovers: The Role of Advisers in Mongolia in the 1920s and in Eastern Europe after World War II." *East European Quarterly,* vol. 28, no. 4, 1994.
4. Myadar, Orhon. "In the Soviet Shadow: Soviet Colonial Politics in Mongolia." *Inner Asia,* vol. 19, no. 1, 2017.
5. Kuromiya, Hiroaki. "Stalin's Great Terror and the Asian Nexus." *Europe-Asia Studies,* vol. 66, no. 5, 2014.
6. "Communist Dictatorship in Mongolia (1921–1990)." *Mongolia | Communist Crimes.*

Exhibit 24. The Khanty. 1931–1933
1. Первый Библиотечный (Pervyi Bibliotechnyi). "Booktrailer Based on the Novel by E.D. Aipin 'Mother of God in the Bloody Snows'." [Rus.] *YouTube,* 29 March 2022.
2. Piskunov, Sergey; Rumyantsev, Vyacheslav. "Kazym uprisings of 1931–1934. The Timeline." [Rus.] *Khronos.*
3. Свободная школа Сопротивления (Free School of Civil Movement Resistance). "The Kazym Uprising. A Lecture by Alexei Grigorjevich Tavrizov." *YouTube,* 26 November 2013.
4. Ernykhova, O. D. *Kazym Rebellion (On the History of the Kazym Rebellion of 1933–1934).* [Rus.] Yugra State University, 2010.
5. Ernykhova, O. D. "Oral Stories of Residents about the Destruction of the Kazym Uprising of 1933–34 and Its Consequences." [Rus.] *Traditional and Innovative Science: History, Current Status, Prospects: Collection of Articles,* vol. 3, 2017.

Exhibit 25. The Dolgans. 1932
1. Sheksheev, Alexander. "Maut for Russians. Uprising in Taimyr." [Rus.] *Sibirskie ogni,* no. 12, December 2021.
2. Bicheool, Vladimir. "Colonization in Taimyr: Socio-cultural Consequences." [Rus.] *Znanie-Ponimanie-Umenie, Knowledge. Understanding. Skill,* 2013.
3. Zamarayeva, Yulia S., et al. "Taymyr Reindeer Herding as a Branch of the Economy and a Fundamental Social Identification Practice for Indigenous Peoples of the Siberian Arctic." *Mediterranean Journal of Social Sciences,* vol. 6, no. 3, 2015.

Exhibit 26. The Nenets. 1934–1943
1. Vallikivi, Laur. "Two Wars in Conflict: Resistance among Nenets Reindeer Herders in the 1940s." *The Northern Peoples and States: Changing Relationships. Studies in Folk Culture,* vol. 5, 2005.
2. Britskaya, Tatiana. "Cold Colonization in Rus-

sia's Arctic." *Transitions*, 13 December 2021.

Exhibit 27. Poland. 1937–1947

1. Kuromiya, Hiroaki. "The Baltic and Arctic Areas under Stalin. Ethnic Minorities in the Great Soviet Terror of 1937–38." *International Research Group. Abstracts of Presentations. Japan and Soviet National Minorities: Missing Links*, Umea, 25–26 January 2011.
2. "Mass Repressions against Polish." [Rus.] *Program of the Memorial Group*.
3. "The 'Polish Operation' of the NKVD." *Institute of National Remembrance and Mieroszewski Centre*.
4. Zychowicz, Piotr. "The Polish Operation." *Institute of National Remembrance*, 03 March 2021.
5. Snyder, Timothy. "Hitler vs. Stalin: Who Was Worse?" *The New York Review*, 27 January 2011.
6. Tuszynski, Marek, and Dale F. Denda. "Soviet War Crimes against Poland during the Second World War and Its Aftermath: A Review of the Factual Record and Outstanding Questions." *The Polish Review*, vol. 44, no. 2, 1999.
7. "To Inhuman Land — Soviet Deportations of Poles to Siberia." [Pól.] *Institute of National Remembrance*.
8. Ostrowska, Joanna; Zaremba, Marcin. "The Red Army Soldiers Spread Fear. Women Were Afraid of Rape." [Pol.] *Polityka*, 7 March 2009.
9. Snyder, Timothy. *Bloodlands: Europe between Hitler and Stalin*. Basic Books (AZ), 2010.
10. "Collected Content: The Cursed Soldiers." *Institute of National Remembrance*.
11. Gorski, Slawomir. *Last Hope / Ostatnia nadzieja*. TVP SA, 2014.
12. Lisak, Mateusz. "The Kielce Pogrom and the Post-War Period in Selected non-Polish Publications." *Institute of National Remembrance*, 4 March 2021.
13. "Rigged Elections — 19 January 1947." *Institute of National Remembrance*, 4 March 2021.
14. Plokhy, Serhii M. *Yalta: The Price of Peace*. Penguin, 2011.

Exhibit 28. Finland. 1939–1940

1. Kenneth, Laurance. "Finnish Democratic Republic — An Obstacle to Peace." *Finland at War*, 04 December 2019.
2. Michel, Casey. "The Lesson Stalin Could Teach Putin about Invading a Neighbor." *The Politico Magazine*, 14 February 2022.
3. Tanner, Väinö. *The Winter War: Finland against Russia, 1939–1940*. Stanford University Press, 1957.
4. Maria [@vinokcollective]. "Russian Terror: Finland Edition & Lessons for Ukraine". *Instagram*, 7 May 2022.
5. Burtsev, Dmytro [@ukrainianvoices.tw]. "History Repeating: Soviet-Finish War and the Russian Invasion of Ukraine." *Instagram*, 2 September 2022.
6. Pyvovarov, Serhii; Spirin, Yevhen. "82 Years Ago the USSR Attacked Finland. The Soviet Union Hoped for a Quick and Easy Victory, but Eventually Lost More than a Hundred Thousand Soldiers in Three Months. We Recall the Winter War in Archive Photos." *Babel*, 30 November 2021.
7. Engle, Eloise, and Lauri Paananen. *The Winter War: The Soviet Attack on Finland, 1939–1940*. Stackpole Books, 1992.

Exhibit 29. Estonia, Latvia, and Lithuania. 1939–1956

1. Radio Free Europe / Radio Liberty. "Molotov-Ribbentrop: The Pact That Changed Europe's Borders." *YouTube*, 7 November 2019.
2. Annus, Epp, ed. *Coloniality, Nationality, Modernity: A Postcolonial View on Baltic Cultures under Soviet Rule*. Routledge, 2018.
3. "Memorial to the Victims of Communism." *Estonian Institute of Historical Memory*.
4. Hiio, Toomas. "Phase I : The Soviet Occupation of Estonia in 1940–1941." *Estonian International Commission for the Investigation of Crimes Against Humanity*.
5. "Communist Dictatorship in Estonia. The Soviet Occupation (1940–1941; 1944–1991)." *Estonia | Communist Crimes*.
6. "Communist Dictatorship in Latvia. The Soviet Occupation (1940–1941; 1944–1991)." *Latvia | Communist Crimes*.
7. Sagatienė, Dovilė. "The Debate about Soviet Genocide in Lithuania in the Case Law of The European Court of Human Rights." *Nationalities*

Papers, vol. 49, no. 4, 2021.
8. "Communist Dictatorship in Lithuania. The Soviet Occupation (1940–1941; 1944–1991)." *Lithuania | Communist Crimes.*
9. Kurvet-Käosaar, Leena. "Imagining an Hospitable Community in the Deportation Narratives of Baltic Women." *Prose Studies,* vol. 26, no. 1–2, 2003.
10. Radio Free Europe / Radio Liberty. "'Undesirable Elements': How Stalin Deported Nearly 100,000 From The Baltics In Operation 'Priboi'". *YouTube,* 25 March 2019.
11. Davoliūtė, Violeta, and Tomas Balkelis, eds. *Narratives of Exile and Identity: Soviet Deportation Memoirs from the Baltic States.* Central European University Press, 2018.
12. Budrytė, Dovilė. "Experiences of Collective Trauma and Political Activism: A Study of Women 'Agents of Memory' in Post-Soviet Lithuania." *Journal of Baltic Studies,* vol. 41, no. 3, 2010.
13. "Home." *The Genocide and Resistance Research Centre of Lithuania (LGGRTC).*
14. "Documentary examines the fight of the 'Forest Brothers'." *LSM.lv.* 9 October 2020.
15. Rotten Tomatoes Indie. "The Invisible Front Official Trailer 1 (2014) — Documentary HD." *YouTube,* 3 November 2014.

Exhibit 30. Romania. 1940–1958
1. "The Genocide of Romanians in Northern Bukovina. Radio Romania International." *Radio Romania International,* 02 May 2016.
2. Casu, Igor. "Stalinist Terror in Soviet Moldavia, 1940–1953." *Stalinist Terror in Eastern Europe,* Manchester, 2010.
3. Siscanu, Elena. *Basarabia sub regimul bolsevic: (1940–1952).* Semne, 1998.
4. Iamandi, Ionut. "The Red Army Rapes." *Veridica,* 05 March 2021.
5. Constantinescu, Octavia. "The Russian Embassy Mystifies History: Soviet Soldiers did not Commit Atrocities in Romania." [Rom.] *Reacția MAE,* 30 December 2018.
6. Popa, Florina. "A Form of Post-war Cooperation – SOVROM." *Challenges of the Knowledge Society,* 2019.
7. Petrescu, Dacinia Crina, Ruxandra Malina Petrescu-Mag, and Ancuta Radu Tenter. "The Little Chernobyl of Romania: The Legacy of a Uranium Mine as Negotiation Platform for Sustainable Development and the Role of New Ethics." *Journal of Agricultural and Environmental Ethics,* no. 32, 2019.
8. Ciobanu, Monica. "Remembering the Romanian Anti-Communist Armed Resistance: An Analysis of Local Lived Experience." *Eurostudia,* vol. 10, no. 1, 2015.
9. Boldur-Lățescu, Gheorghe. *The Communist Genocide in Romania.* Nova Publishers, 2005.
10. "The Tismaneanu Commission Presents the Final Report on Romanian Communism." [Rom.] *Wilson Center,* 18 December 2006.
11. "Communist Dictatorship in Romania (1947–1989)." *Romania | Communist Crimes.*

Exhibit 31. Bulgaria. 1944–1946
1. "Communist Dictatorship in Bulgaria (1944–1989)." *Bulgaria | Communist Crimes.*
2. Leviev-Sawyer, Clive. "75 Years On, Bulgaria Deeply Divided over Soviet Army Invasion." *The Sofia Globe,* 09 September 2019.
3. "Bulgaria Scolds Russian Narrative on Soviet Role in Liberating Europe." *Radio Free Europe / Radio Liuberty,* 04 September 2019.
4. Kolev, Yoan. "1946: Third Bulgarian Kingdom Ends with a Referendum." *Radio Bulgaria,* 23 August 2014.
5. "Bulgaria Proposes Posthumous State Honours for Anti-communist Guerrilla Fighters." *The Sofia Globe,* 23 November 2016.
6. Voskresenski, Valentin. "The Goryani Movement against the Communist Regime in Bulgaria (1944–1956): Prerequisites, Resistance, Consequences." *Violent Resistance,* 2020.

Exhibit 32. Hungary. 1944–1956
1. Kay, Alex, et al (ed.). "Soviet Occupation of Romania, Hungary, and Austria 1944/45–1948/49." *Central European University Press,* 2015.
2. "Double Occupation Exhibition." *House of Terror Museum.*
3. Stark, Tamás. "'Malenki Robot' — Hungarian Forced Labourers in the Soviet Union (1944–1955)." *Minorities Research,* no. 7, 2005.
4. Gál, Mária; Attila Gajdos Balogh; Ferenc Imreh.

The White Book. Atrocities against Hungarians in the Autumn of 1944 (In Transylvania, Romania). Barna Bodó, Rmdsz (Dahr) Kolozsvár, 1995.
5. Várdy, Agnes Huszár. "Forgotten Victims of World War II: Hungarian Women in Soviet Forced Labor Camps." *DEP*, no. 7, 2002.
6. Borhi, László. *Hungary in the Cold War, 1945–1956: Between the United States and the Soviet Union.* Central European University Press, 2004.
7. "Communist Takeover of Hungary 1946–1949." *The Institute for the History of the 1956 Hungarian Revolution*, 10 December 2003.
8. Parsons, Nicholas T. "Narratives of 1956." *The Hungarian Quarterly*, no. 186, 2007.
9. Gutterman, Ivan. "Remembering the 1956 Hungarian Uprising." *Radio Free Europe / Radio Liberty*, 23 October 2019.
10. Pető, Andrea. "Roots of Illiberal Memory Politics: Remembering Women in the 1956 Hungarian Revolution." *Baltic Worlds*, vol. 4, 2017.

Exhibit 33. Czechia and Slovakia. 1945–1968

1. Gottwald, Klement. "1945–1948: From Liberation to Stalinism." *Radio Prague International*, 1 April 2020.
2. "Communist Dictatorship in Czechoslovakia (1948–1989)." *Czech Republic (Czechoslovakia) | Communist Crimes.*
3. CriticalPast. "Czechoslovak Coup with Communists Coming to Power; anti-Communist demonstrations… HD Stock Footage." *YouTube*, 5 April 2014.
4. Guryčová, Kristýna. "The Investigation into the Death of Jan Masaryk Is Over. The Police Were Unable to Prove the Murder Unequivocally." [Czech.] *iRozhlas*, 8 March 2021.
5. Valenta, Jiri. "From Prague to Kabul: The Soviet Style of Invasion." *International Security*, vol. 5, no. 2, 1980.
6. "The Soviet Invasion of Czechoslovakia: A Russian Propaganda Poster Seeking to Defuse Popular Resistance." [Archive].
7. Chapple, Amos. "Invasion. The Crushing of the Prague Spring." *Radio Free Europe / Radio Liberty*, 10 August 2018.
8. Tait, Robert. "Prague 1968: Lost Images of the Day that Freedom Died." *The Guardian*, 19 August 2018.
9. Navrátil, Jaromír (ed.). *The Prague Spring, 1968.* Central European University Press, 2006.
10. Canby, Peter. "The Day the Soviets Arrived to Crush the Prague Spring, in Rarely Seen Photos." *The New Yorker*, 26 August 2018.
11. Fraňková, Ruth. "Historians Pin down Number of 1968 Invasion Victims." *Radio Prague International*, 18 August 2017.

Exhibit 34. Germany. 1953

1. "The timeline of the June 17–18 Uprising." *17Juni53.de. Bundeszentrale für politische Bildung, Deutschlandradio, Zentrum für Zeithistorische Forschung Potsdam*, 2004.
2. Applebaum, Anne. *Iron Curtain: The Crushing of Eastern Europe, 1944–1956.* Anchor, 2012.
3. British Pathè. "Dramatic Scenes — Berlin Riots (1953)." *YouTube*, 13 April 2004.
4. Glees, Anthony. "The 1953 Revolt in East Germany: Violence and Betrayal." *OpenDemocracy*, 30 June 2003.
5. Geerling, Wayne, Gary B. Magee, and Russell Smyth. "Occupation, Reparations, and Rebellion: The Soviets and the East German Uprising of 1953." *Journal of Interdisciplinary History*, vol. 52, no. 2, 2021.
6. Dale, Gareth. "'Like Wildfire?' The East German Uprising of 1953." Debatte. *Review of Contemporary German Affairs*, vol. 11, no. 2, 2003.

Exhibit 35. Afghanistan. 1979–1989

1. Azmi, M. Raziullah. "Russian Expansion in Central Asia and the Afghan Question (1865–85)." *Pakistan Horizon*, vol. 37, no. 3, 1984.
2. Assifi, Abdul Tawab. "The Russian Rope: Soviet Economic Motives and the Subversion of Afghanistan." *World Affairs*, vol. 145, no. 3, 1982.
3. Savranskaya, Svetlana; Blanton, Tom (ed.). "The Soviet Invasion of Afghanistan, 1979: Not Trump's Terrorists, Nor Zbig's Warm Water Ports." *National Security Archive*, 29 January 2019.
4. Reuveny, Rafael, and Aseem Prakash. "The Afghanistan War and the Breakdown of the Soviet Union." *Review of International Studies*, vol. 25, no. 4, 1999.

Exhibit 36. Qazaqstan. 1986

1. Tyan, Alexandra; Thompson, Caitlin. "An

Anti-Soviet Protest in Kazakhstan Haunts the Country's Current Unrest." *CodaStory*, 7 January 2022.
2. Aytenova, Alfiya; Kairatuly, Samat. "Jeltoqsan–1986: Evaluation, Causes, and Representation in Art." [Qaz.] *Al-Farabi*, vol. 76, no. 4, 2021.
3. Putz, Catherine. "1986: Kazakhstan's Other Independence Anniversary." *The Diplomat*, 16 December 2016.
4. Гиперборей (GYPERBOREJ). "Zheltoksan 1986. 'Chronicle of an Unannounced Demonstration'. Documentary. Directed by Asiya Baigozhina. English Subs." *YouTube*, 16 December 2022.
5. "December 1986: How It Was – Special Project of 'Zheltoksan-86'." [Rus.] Exclusive, 20 December 2016.
6. Yelim-ai Education. "dudeontheguitar & Hey Monro - OTAN ANA [MV]." [Qaz.] *YouTube*, 16 December 2022.

Exhibit 37. Sakartvelo (Georgia). 1989–1993
1. "Georgia: 33 Years since April 9 Tragedy, when Soviet Army Massacred Peaceful Demonstrators in Tbilisi." *Jam News*, 9 April 2022.
2. Fain, Stephanie. "Russian Power Brokering, Peacemaking, and Meddling in the Georgian-Abkhaz Conflict." *LBJ Journal of Public Affairs*, no. 27, 2005.
3. Sayin, Fatih, and Valeri Modebadze. "The Role of Russia in Provoking Conflict between Georgians and Abkhazians." *Uluslararası Alanya İşletme Fakültesi Dergisi*, vol. 7, no. 3, 2015.
4. Goltz, Thomas. "Letter from Eurasia: The Hidden Russian Hand." *Foreign Policy*, no. 92, 1993.
5. Chapple, Amos. "The Tbilisi War: Then and Now." *Radio Free Europe / Radio Liberty*, 21 December 2021.
6. Mchedlishvili, Zviad; Chumburidze, Giorgi. "Tbilisi's 1991–1992 War: A Ruthless Conflict that Had to Be Fought, Veterans Agree." *Current Time*, 22 December 2021.

Exhibit 38. Azerbaijan. 1989–1991
1. Musavi, Nika. "Remembering Baku's 'Black January': 'Tanks Were Crushing and Shooting at Everyone'." *Current Time*, 29 January 2020.
2. Abilov, Shamkhal, and Ismayil Isayev. "The National Revival in Azerbaijan Prior to the Fall of the Soviet Union and 'black January'." *"Azerbaijani" and Beyond*, 2017.
3. Betts, Wendy. "Third Party Mediation: An Obstacle to Peace in Nagorno Karabakh." *SAIS Review (1989–2003)*, vol. 19, no. 2, 1999.

Exhibit 39. Lithuania. 1990–1991
1. Zverko, Natalija. "How Lithuania's Minorities Joined the Fight for Independence in 1991." *LRT.lt*, 13 January 2022.
2. Cosman, Catherine. "Glasnost in Jeopardy: Human Rights in the USSR." *Human Rights Watch*, 1991.
3. Music Information Centre Lithuania. "Lithuanian radio announcement to the world on the night of January 13, 1991." *YouTube*, 13 January 2021.
4. Lietuvos nacionalinis radijas ir televizija. "U Lithuania January events archive." *YouTube*, 12 January 2016.
5. "About Website." *The Nation's Memory: The 13th of January. Martynas Mažvydas National Library of Lithuania*, 2006.
6. "Journalist Recalls the Moment When Soviet Troops Stormed TV Studio on January 13, 1991." *The Lithuania Tribune*, 13 January 2016.

Exhibit 40. Latvia. 1990–1991
1. Dobbs, Michael. "Latvia Calls Bombings Pretext for Soviet Takeover." *The Washington Post*, 19 December 1990.
2. "Adoption of the Declaration of Independence, the Barricades (1990–1991)." *Ministry of Defence of the Republic of Latvia*.
3. Zaltāns, Kaspars. "Latvia's Barricades of Freedom – What Do They Mean 25 Years On?" *Deep Baltic*, 8 March 2016.
4. "Five Stories from the 1991 Rīga Barricades." *LSM.lv*, 20 January 2020.
5. "See: 25 Historic Photos from Riga during the Barricades." *LSM.lv*, 19 January 2018.
6. "Video: The Defense of Freedom during the Time of the Barricades." *LSM.lv*, 27 January 2020.
7. "Home." *Museum of the Barricades of 1991*.

Exhibit 41. Estonia. 1991
1. Schwab, Katharine. "A Country Created through Music." *The Atlantic*, 12 November 2015.
2. Tusty, Maureen Castle; Tusty, James. *The Sing-

ing Revolution. A single nation. A million voices. The fall of an empire. A Documentary, 2006.

Exhibit 42. Moldova. 1992

1. Plokhy, Serhii. *The Last Empire: The Final Days of the Soviet Union.* Basic Books (A-Z), 2015.

2. "Military Occupation of Moldova by Russia." *The Rule of Law in Armed Conflicts Project (RULAC) of the Geneva Academy of International Humanitarian Law and Human Rights,* 2 February 2022.

3. Całus, Kamil. "Gagauzia: Growing Separatism in Moldova?" *OSW Commentary,* no. 129, 2014.

4. Yarmolenko, Oleksiy; Spirin, Yevhen. "29 Years Ago Russia Forced Moldova to Freeze the War in Transnistria. Since then Chisinau Lived with the Occupied Territory, Maintaining Economic and Social Ties with It. And All Started because of Language and Russian Army." *Babel,* 21 August 2021.

5. Munteanu, Angela, Igor Munteanu. "Transnistria: A Paradise for Vested Interests." *SEER: Journal for Labour and Social Affairs in Eastern Europe,* vol. 10, no. 4, 2007.

6. Nagashima, Toru. "Russia's Passportization Policy toward Unrecognized Republics: Abkhazia, South Ossetia, and Transnistria." *Problems of Post-Communism,* vol. 66, no. 3, 2019.

Exhibit 43. Tajikistan. 1992–1997

1. Mamadaliev, Inomjon. "The Tragedy of Colonialism — Tajik Phenomenon: The History of Tajiks at the Second Half of XIX – Beginning of XX Centuries." *JSIS University of Washington,* 2016.

2. Kassymbekova, Botakoz. *Despite Cultures: Early Soviet Rule in Tajikistan.* University of Pittsburgh Press, 2016.

3. Ubaidulloev, Zubaidullo. "The Russian-Soviet Legacies in Reshaping the National Territories in Central Asia: A Catastrophic Case of Tajikistan." *Journal of Eurasian Studies,* vol. 6, no. 1, 2015.

4. "Minorities at Risk Project." *Chronology for Russians in Tajikistan,* 2004.

5. AP Archive. "Tajikistan: Russian Troops Clash with Rebels." [Rus.] *YouTube,* 21 July 2015.

6. Sobiri, Bakhtiyor. "The Long Echo of Tajikistan's Civil War." *OpenDemocracy,* 23 June 2017.

7. Marat, Erica. *The Military and the State in Central Asia: From Red Army to Independence.* Routledge, 2009.

Exhibit 44. Ichkeria (Chechnya). 1991–2000

1. Avtorkhanov, Abdurakhman. *Kremlin Empire: Soviet Type of Colonialism.* [Rus.] Prometheus Verlag, 1988.

2. Casula, Philipp. "Between 'Ethnocide' and 'Genocide': Violence and Otherness in the Coverage of the Afghanistan and Chechnya Wars." *The Return to War and Violence,* vol. 43, no. 5, 2017.

3. Galeotti, Mark. *Russia's Wars in Chechnya 1994–2009.* Osprey Publishing, 2014.

4. Opryshchenko, Anastasiya. "Russian Federation Has Been Waging Wars throughout All Its History — Always Insidiously and Vilely." *Zaborona,* 11 April 2022.

5. UATV English. "Putin's Colonialist Wars: Civilian Casualties and Atrocities in Chechnya and Ukraine Compared." *YouTube,* 7 August 2022.

6. Bouckaert, Peter. "War Crimes in Chechnya and the Response of the West. Testimony before the Senate Committee on Foreign Relations." *Human Rights Watch,* 29 February 2000.

7. le Huérou, Anne, and Amandine Regamey. "Massacres of Civilians in Chechnya." *SciencesPo,* 9 March 2015.

8. Chapple, Amos. "'Welcome To Hell, Part II': The Second Chechen War." *Radio Free Europe / Radio Liberty,* 1 October 2019.

9. Michel, Casey. "Decolonize Russia." *The Atlantic,* 27 May 2022.

10. "Russia / Chechnya." *Human Rights Watch,* 1997.

11. Reinke, Sarah. "Schleichender Völkermord in Tschetschenien." [Ger.] *GfbV,* 2005.

12. Engelhardt, Anna. "War by Any Other Name: Patterns of Russian Colonialism." *The Funambulist,* no. 62, 2022.

13. Wilhelmsen, Julie. "Colonized Children: Chechnya in Russia." *Kinship in International Relations,* Chapter 6, Routledge, 2018.

14. Campana, Aurélie. "The Effects of War on the Chechen National Identity Construction." *National Identities,* vol. 8, no. 2, 2006.

Exhibit 45. Sakartvelo (Georgia). 2008

1. Kandelaki, Giorgi. "Georgia's Rose Revolution.

A Participant's Perspective." *United States Institute of Peace,* July 2006.
2. Crosby, Alan. "She Coined the Catchphrase: Looking Back on the 'Rose Revolution'." *Radio Free Europe / Radio Liberty,* 23 November 2018.
3. Beehner, Lionel, et al. "Analyzing the Russian Way of War: Evidence from the 2008 Conflict with Georgia." *Modern War Institute,* 2018.
4. Toria, Malkhaz. "The Soviet Occupation of Georgia in 1921 and the Russian – Georgian War of August 2008: Historical Analogy as a Memory Project." *The Making of Modern Georgia, 1918–2012,* 2014.
5. "Consequences of Russian Aggression in Georgia. Basic Facts." *The Ministry of Foreign Affairs of Georgia.*
6. "Ethnic Cleansing of Georgians Resulted from Russian Invasion and Occupation since August 8, 2008." *Ministry of Justice of Georgia,* 6 October 2008.
7. Harding, Luke. "Russia Committed Human Rights Violation in Georgia War, ECHR Rules." *The Guardian,* 21 January 2021.
8. Rondeli, Alexander. "The Russian-Georgian War and Its Implications for Georgia's State Building." *The Making of Modern Georgia 1918–2012,* 2014.

Exhibit 46. Ukraine. 2014–2022
1. Plokhy, Serhii. *The Frontline: Essays on Ukraine's Past and Present.* Harvard University Press, 2022.
2. Plokhy, Serhii. *The Gates of Europe: A History of Ukraine.* Basic Books (A-Z), 2015.
3. Hromadske. "Donetsk Spring. The Fight for the Homeland." *YouTube,* 9 May 2016.
4. Kuromiya, Hiroaki. "The Future of the Donbas: Lessons from Russia's Past." *Krytyka,* January 2021.
5. Gumenyuk, Nataliya. *Lost Island. A Book of Reporting from the Occupied Crimea.* [Ukr.] Staryi Lev, 2020.
6. "'You Do Not Come Back from War': How the Journalist Valeriia Burlakova Volunteered to Serve and Later Became a Writer." *Hromadske,* 25 November 2021.
7. Kutiepov, Bohdan. "'Elvis' on the Front Line." *Hromadske,* 11 November 2014.
8. Romanenko, Maria. "Blood, Sweat, and Tears in a Record-Breaking Ukrainian War Film." *Hromadske,* 15 January 2018.
9. Tumakova, Irina. "An Open Secret: How Russia Hides Its Soldiers Killed in the Donbas." *Hromadske / Novaya Gazeta,* 1 August 2018.
10. "No Way Home for Residents of Ukraine's 'Gray Zone'." *Hromadske,* 26 January 2018.
11. "In East Ukraine, Locals and Aid Agencies Struggle Through War's Fourth Year." *Hromadske,* 14 February 2018.
12. Stanko, Anastasiya. "Eastern Ukraine. Before the Front Lines." *Hromadske,* 6 November 2014.
13. Quinn, Allison. "We Have Failed Ukraine — and All Those Erased by Putin." *The Daily Beast,* 24 February 2022.
14. Yermak, Andriy. "The Global System Has Failed. Ukraine Is Showing the World How to Build a Better One." *Time,* 28 April 2022.

Exhibit 47. Syria. 2015–2023
1. Dettmer, Jamie. "Russia Expands Military Facilities in Syria." *Voice of America,* 12 May 2021.
2. Birnbaum, Michael. "The Secret Pact between Russia and Syria that Gives Moscow Carte Blanche." *The Washington Post,* 15 January 2016.
3. Starr, Terrell Jermaine. "Why Progressives Should Help Defend Ukraine." *The Foreign Policy,* 11 February 2022.
4. Hamdo, Ahmad Haj. "Lessons Learned from Syrian Journalists Investigating Russian War Crimes." *Global Investigative Journalism Network,* 6 April 2022.
5. Borger, Julian. "Russia Committed War Crimes in Syria, Finds UN report." *The Guardian,* 2 March 2020.
6. "Russia/Syria: War Crimes in Month of Bombing Aleppo." *Human Rights Watch,* 1 December 2016.
7. "Accountability for Russian crimes in Syria and Ukraine." *Syria Justice and Accountability Centre,* 18 March 2022.
8. "Syrian Revolution 11 Years on | SOHR Documents by Names nearly 161,000 Civilian Deaths, including 40,500 Children and Women." *The Syrian Observatory For Human Rights,* 15 March 2022.
9. "Syria Emergency Factsheet." *UNHCR.*

10. Karam, Zeina; Mroue, Bassem, Naddaff, Aj. "How Russia's Intervention in Syria Provided Blueprint for Ukraine Invasion." *The Times of Israel,* 1 March 2022.

11. Jalani, Marwan Safar. "The Russian Invasion of Ukraine Happened because the World Gave Vladimir Putin a Free Pass in Syria." *Atlantic Council,* 9 March 2022.

12. Smith, Amelia. "The War on Syria Emboldened Russia and Its Relentless Targeting of Civilians in Ukraine." *Middle East Monitor,* 1 March 2022.

Exhibit 48. Ukraine 2022 – TBC

1. Radynski, Oleksiy. "The Case Against the Russian Federation." *E-flux Journal,* no. 125, 2022.
2. Engelhardt, Anna. "The Futures of Russian Decolonization." *Strelka Mag,* 18 March 2022.
3. Timothy Snyder. "The War in Ukraine Is a Colonial War." *The New Yorker,* 28 April 2022.
4. Zabuzhko, Oksana. "The Problem with Russia is Russia." *The New York Times,* 20 February 2023.
5. Hook, Kristina. "Why Russia's War in Ukraine Is a Genocide." *Foreign Affairs,* 28 July 2022.
6. "Seven Countries Have Already Recognised Russia's War Against Ukraine As Genocide." *Promote Ukraine,* 29 May 2022.
7. Apt, Clara. "Russia's Eliminationist Rhetoric Against Ukraine: A Collection." *Just Security,* 29 June 2023.
8. Whatcott, Elizabeth. "Compilation of Countries' Statements Calling Russian Actions in Ukraine 'Genocide'." *Just Security,* 20 May 2022.
9. Chernov, Mstyslav, director. *20 Days in Mariupol.* 2023.
10. Kvedaravicius, Mantas, director. *Mariupolis 2.* 2022.
11. Ponomarenko, Roman. "Army of Marauders: The Long History of Russian Military Looting, Pillaging, and Stealing." *Euromaidan Press,* 28 June 2022.
12. Blinken, Antony J. "Russia's 'Filtration' Operations, Forced Disappearances, and Mass Deportations of Ukrainian Citizens." *U.S. Department of State,* 13 July 2022.
13. Hinton, Alexander. "Russia's Mass Kidnappings of Ukrainians Are a Page out of a Wartime Playbook — and Evidence of Genocide." *The Conversation,* 20 July 2022.
14. Amelina, Victoria. "Victoria Amelina: Ukraine and the Meaning of Home." *The Guardian,* 06 July 2023.

Russian Colonialism

	ist publishing
Author:	Maksym Eristavi
Art director:	Sergiy Maidukov
Artists:	Sergiy Maidukov, Alisa Gots, Nikita Kravtsov,
	Nataliia Kozeko, Danyl Shtangeev,
	Natasha Steshenko, Ave Libertatemaveamor
Editing:	Zoe Turner
Proofreading:	Iryna Kurhanska, Tom Giuretis
Design and layout:	Ostap Yashchuk
ist publishing project team:	Kateryna Nosko, Anastasia Leonova
Typeface:	Gill Sans Nova, Noto Sans
Print:	ELEKTROPRODUCT Kft.
	3500 copies
	4th edition
Publisher:	Private entrepreneur Leonova Anastasia Romanivna
	ist publishing — comercial naming
	e-mail: team@istpublishing.org

Certificate of inclusion of the subject of publishing in the State Register
of Publishers, Manufacturers, and Distributors of Publishing Products
DK № 5289 dated 18.02.2017

ist publishing news on the site:
www.istpublishing.org

This book may not be used in whole or in part in any form without
the written consent of ist publishing.